Women's Ways With Fire

Transforming Self in the Heart of Nature

ISMANA CARNEY, PhD

outskirtspress
DENVER, COLORADO

Contents

INTRODUCTION

THIS BOOK IS about a small human and nonhuman community of Fire, trees, rocks, herbs and honey, unseen but felt entities, the spoken word, and all creatures great and small. Its literary infrastructure is not linear but, rather like a mandala, it is circular, multidimensional, and dynamic with no reference necessarily to rational definitions of time and space. It is about the process of individuation as articulated by Swiss psychiatrist and founder of analytical psychology Carl Jung. It also describes sacred relationship to and with Earth.

Deep ecologist, pacifist, and Buddhist philosopher Joanna Macy reminds us of the profound wisdom of knowing in the soul, an eternal bond with creation, and of having the ability, whether we know it or not, to love things and our Selves back to life. She also discusses the timeless value of world indigenous ceremonial traditions that hold to an imperative that is often verbalized by Anne Marie Sayers, Tribal chairperson of the Costanoan-Ohlone at Indian Canyon in Hollister, California. At numerous events, Anne Marie talks about her great-grandmother, who always insisted, "When the sacred dances, the rituals, and the ceremonies end, so too will the world."

It is important to emphasize that the Earth-centered rites I am speaking of function in and are reflective of the presence of the Divine. In other words, they are holy acts. We imagine creatively, and in the process, image Earth and our relationship to and with her in an endless variety of inspired ways depending on our history, culture, and soul disposition.

This work is a personal response to this view that the natural world is sacramental to the soul. Sacramental in the sense that Earth and all her life forms, her Nature, are inseparable at the most fundamental level. Knowingly responding to the dynamic relations between them thus becomes critical, in particular for humans, to repairing the ever-widening rift between us and this beloved life-giving and life-sustaining blue planet. It is imperative that we recall, retrieve, and once again live with the reality of which Jung reminds us: Earth too has a soul. Her Nature is the Divine manifested. She is Spirit, a manifestation of the Divine translated into this lovely fragment of creation we know as our world.

I believe that Earth, as an ensouled being, is, by definition, intelligent, intentional, self-aware, purposeful, and of ultimate significance. If we accept this premise as a foundation on which to form a living relationship to and with her, we can begin the process of rearticulating in both concrete and personalized terms the symbiotic interrelationship between all beings. Only then can we begin to, in depth-psychologist Lionel Corbett's words, "repair the split which has bedeviled our culture."

This book is grounded in Jung's nature psychology, itself based on his own lifelong interaction with Nature as a sacred and intelligent being, and in my own personal and abiding relationship to and with Earth. I have chosen to capitalize the words Nature and Earth to indicate Earth's status as both a material and a soulful entity who articulates the presence of the Divine in the language of her own Nature, a language we may understand through the conscious observation of naturally occurring synchronicities, signs, and symbols. Additionally, words that in normal circumstances would not be capitalized but are in this work refer to their deeper sense of the meaning. They may also refer to objects, symbols, archetypes, or persons who signify the presence and action of the Divine in human affairs. For instance, when I capitalize the word Self, I am referring to that aspect of ourselves that is referenced by the soul, our higher or inner Self, the core of human being, whose natural and unswerving orientation is toward the Divine.

We may also understand the Self as the impersonal I, or that aspect Jung refers to as the archetype of wholeness. Jungian scholar and psychoanalyst Edward Edinger elaborates the I as that sense of Self that is placed beyond the ego-personality and is the ordering and unifying center of the soul in the same way that the "ego is the center of the conscious personality." In contrast to my ego-driven self, I experience my Self as soul referenced and transcendent; an eternal being in her own right embodied temporarily in human form. She steadies me as I tread the pilgrim's path leading ultimately to my own point of origin in the Divine. If you have experienced a higher sense of yourself that is able to stand above or beyond your own experience, watching, and witnessing, providing an objective perspective so that you can resolve or reconcile or come to a deeper understanding of the situation at hand, then you know your Self.

She, my Self, also serves as the axis around which both my inner and outer worlds revolve. From my own soul's perspective, this axis is a microcosmic mirroring of the axis mundi envisioned anciently and symbolically as the Tree of Life or the World Tree: a bridge-being between all worlds. It is my soul's identification of her own Selfhood within a framework of interaction with the Divine. In Hinduism, it is where the Atman, the true Self, comes face to face with the Brahman, the Source of all Existence, realizing in that instance her own reflected divinity.

This is not to diminish the profound inherence, integrity, and soulful aspects of other dimensions of human being such as ego, intellect, heart, body, instinct, and consciousness. It is to say that in the deepest center of my being, there is something I identify as Self that is mysteriously separate and sacred, and yet, as the Prophet Muhammad insists in the Holy Quran, closer to me than my own jugular vein. She is a vibrant, intentional, and radiant entity not necessarily related to any other aspect of my human being. When the body dies, she simply slips away, continuing in the enchanting heart of an infinite and eternal mystery.

Jung believed that the soul-referenced Self would reach a certain level of comprehension after which it would no longer have to return in human form. Rather, it would "vanish from the 3-dimensional world and attain Nirvana" depending on the completion or incompletion of the individuation process and how much inner work remained to be done. There is a great and merciful compassion here.

The words Divine, Spirit and God, which I will use interchangeably throughout this work, are also capitalized to signal that deepest of all mysteries: the ultimately unknowable Source of all things. I also choose to identify Earth's inherent nature as female based on a broad array of personal and cultural references and spiritual experiences across space and time.

I am also greatly concerned with what I see as an increasing alienation from our own human natures, and, by extension, from Earth in her own Nature. Jung urges us to live "in modest harmony with Nature," not only as individuals but also as communities and cultures because he understands that a suffering and depleted Earth bespeaks a suffering and depleted humanity.

How do we begin to retrieve a long-lost appreciation and valuation of our Selves and our communities, keeping in mind our symbiotic relationship to Earth? Jung's answer is to urge each of us to embark on a journey of Self discovery, the ultimate goal being to actualize ourselves as centered, fulfilled, and illuminated individuals. He calls this the process of individuation.

Because the individuation process within the context of ritual engagement with Earth is the central motif of this book, a short initial description of the process from Jung's perspective is important. We may understand individuation as a lifelong psychological, emotional, physical, and spiritual process of negotiating the inherent contradictions between the goals of our ego-driven personality and our more intuitive soul-referenced Self as we strive for wholeness, balance, liberation and wisdom.

For many of us, beginning in childhood, our Self, with its divinely sourced creative imagination and unbounded spirit, is almost immediately deprecated, diminished, ridiculed, and finally defeated by parents, family, culture, and life experience. Consequently, for most of us, the awareness of the eternal presence of soul that we are all born with simply fades over time into unreachable depths of being. For those of us whose loss is not total there is a kind of bittersweet mystery lodged in the heart of things that gifts our lives with a nutritive, ironic joy. We experience a knowing at deeper levels of being that our soul remains a powerful presence at work and at play in our lives.

Then there are those, who, in spite of traumatic self-defeating childhood experiences, are able to remain Self-aware. The lived experience for these individuals, in spite of all of life's challenges, only deepens, becoming increasingly complex, and inspired by the constancy of transcendence.

While the ego-driven self is continually informed and shaped by the senses, desires, emotions, rational intellect, history, and cultural influences, the individuating Self must constantly oversee, modify, complement, or compensate, either positively or negatively, the results of our self-centered activities and decisions. Meanwhile, the soul serves as a balancing mechanism in relation to the ego's needs, and is constantly at work advocating for the higher, unselfish goals of the Self. Goals that include an ethically grounded integrity and wholeness of being, functioning in an abiding harmony of relations with all of our self-aspects. We might call this discipline of maintaining equilibrium between order and disorder, kindness and cruelty, love and hate, creativity and stagnation, the whole cycle of life itself, the spiritual practice of the soul.

This is individuation. Depending on one's orientation, it may be understood as a pilgrimage in the true sense of that term: a journey whose mission is sacred leading toward a holy place or object or ultimate state of being. It is a process in which the individual is fully engaged in soul work, whether in a traditional patient-therapist relationship, in the process of self-analysis, or through a life deeply engaged in culturally prescribed spiritual practices. Throughout the book, I will refer to the individuation process synonymously using such terms as Self-discovery, Self-awareness, or the path to transcendence or illumination, among others.

One of several keys to initiating and then sustaining the process of individuation is what Jung calls the transcendent function. The transcendent function activates in various ways. For example, when faced with something that is causing you fear, confusion, pain, and despair it may take the form of a difficult inner conversation or even an outright battle between the personality-driven ego and the soul-referenced Self. The result of this confrontation is critical to understanding what must be done to avoid permanent damage. This is key. It is where critically important information is exchanged between the ego with all its own self-aspects, such as critic, judge, joker and coward, traitor and tyrant etc., and the Self. Alternatively, if you call your Self into a scenario whose resolution requires a higher wisdom, a shot of courage, the steel edge of truth, a measure of love, or a kinder response, the transcendent function may appear in the form of transforming mythological, or archetypal images, symbols, sudden irrefutable insights, dreams, or synchronistic occurrences. Jung calls this the mythopoetic language of the soul. The stories, perspectives, and wisdom traditions contained in these powerful images serve to inform and, maybe more importantly, to provide a metaphysical context within which you may conduct this dire inner conversation and collaborate with the higher Self to creatively and constructively negotiate, mediate, and positively transform the moment.

In everyday terms, individuation is about spending a lifetime getting to know all aspects of your self really well. How do we grow, develop, and evolve as a soul-referenced being keeping the Sacred in mind? How do we protect and guard the Self at all costs? And then, if we lose sight of her, how do we restore the loss? How do we become

Self-aware? How do we cultivate Self-knowledge via the process of individuation? We do this by consciously and courageously surrendering to the *affect,* in other words, the emotional intensity or inner stressors of a given moment. And we need to do this throughout our lives. It is a never-ending journey.

Do you remember your falling dreams? From childhood and into young adulthood I suffered years of falling dreams that occurred in sequential series each lasting for months at a time. They were described by particular images and storylines and ended with me forcing myself to wake up, shivering in a cold sweat, wrapped in a cowl of cowardice. Shameful. Even as a child, I was deeply concerned with being viewed as brave, as invincible.

Finally, in my early twenties, in one particular dream, while I was tumbling headlong into a pitch of infinite black, I said to myself, "To hell with it! I'm not going to fight this! I'm just going to fall and see how this dream will end." It was a point of no return for me. Now this particular sequence of dreams had me falling from the stars or some planet into fathomless dark space with nowhere to run, nowhere to hide, and no gravitational draw on which to cling. Then, in the final dream of this series something wonderful happened. Plunging into space at accelerating speeds, ready to meet the Angel of Death, I was suddenly swept up and experienced being enclosed firmly in the "hands of God" all the while listening intently to the word "beloved" whispered in my ear like a love song caught fast in the rosy, golden light of dawn.

Soon after, I began a new dream series lasting another several years where I was taught to override the fall and to take flight instead. Once I mastered the skill, I flew everywhere at will, sometimes alone, sometimes in good company. I flew across the world, into the universe, into deep space and through time to the beginning and to the end of things. I learned much.

In the final flying dream, I was gifted with an inner message that my training at Dream Flight School was for one great purpose only. That at the moment of my death I will know how to consciously leave my body, making my way with the speed and accuracy of light to the farthest reaches of wherever my destiny will lead.

When we fully and fearlessly surrender to the fall into the dark side of nothing, the aware Self releases irresistible counter energy from within its own heart-of-being. It is a place where the Divine moves in secret intimacy with the soul, and in that sacred union triggers an energy-charge in the soul that ignites flight.

As far as my 'flying' dreams are concerned, we can also say that my longing to overcome a childhood fear of heights and of falling provoked my dreaming self to access integrative and healing images, transforming symbols, and the presence of the Divine. They activated as transcendent functions both within the interior landscape of my being and in my outer, lived life. I am no longer afraid of falling from anything, including Grace, or of dying that way.

᛫᛫᛫᛫

To return to the process of individuation, when the transcendent function, we could also say the soul's messenger, has brought to light an activated complex such as a mother complex or an inferiority complex or a wounded inner child complex, the challenge is for the ego-driven personality to respond in correspondingly appropriate ways. We must allow our inner voices their say. Then, depending on its intensity, the ensuing debate may generate enough creative energy to produce a sudden insight, a profound shift in perspective, or a new level of understanding that is enlightening. The situation to be dealt with can then be reframed and resolved, opening the way for an authentic transformation of being. There is also danger here.

Because, as a consequence we may find ourselves on a path that takes an unexpected turn and leads to a headlong collision with our own Shadow. From a Jungian perspective, the Shadow as a profoundly complex aspect of the Self resides and functions at every level of being, in every moment of our lives. "Everyone carries a Shadow," Jung tells us, "and the less it is embodied in the individual's conscious life, the blacker and denser it is."

Our Shadow aspect may be understood as many things, including those we are not fully conscious of, actively deny or must keep secret because to reveal them might cause madness and mayhem that may prove untenable. On the other hand, if we have been forced by circumstances to conceal important aspects of who we are and with them qualities, talents, abilities and certain measures of radiance, then we may also understand the Shadow as the dark guardian of inner treasures yet to be rediscovered and returned to the bright light of day.

The Shadow's multilayered presence and role in our lives depends on how effectively or ineffectively we have negotiated and resolved our darker life experiences. Inattentiveness, procrastination, dishonesty, denial and repression are all the work of the Shadow.

The process of individuation, in fact any effort to deepen our lived experience, searching for meaning and significance, all this of necessity propels us toward our own Shadow. And we encounter our shaded self when we are in process of a breakdown or when we fall headlong into our own abyss only to come face to face with our own arrogance, laziness, fear, confusion, indecisiveness, undisclosed shame, and self-entrapments. "A man who is possessed by his Shadow," Jung tells us, "is always standing in his own light and falling into his own traps ... living below his own level." This is where the warrior aspect of the Self comes in. Self-evolution more often than not takes place on the battlefields of the human heart where, according to the Russian novelist, Fyodor Dostoyevsky, God and the Devil fight it out for possession of our souls.

Finally, the process of individuation consists of realizing and embracing the fact that we humans are, by nature, multifaceted. We must eventually learn to live among, come to terms with, and be at peace with the multiple selves inside our own skin.

For those of us who have an innate and immediate sense of a living connection with Earth, I believe this inner journey toward discovering and ultimately coming to terms with our Selves can be most powerfully transformative when undertaken within the heart of Nature. This can be done via Earth-centered, ritualized acknowledgments of the relational presence of the Divine in all living things such as the Fire rituals at the solstices and equinoxes so wisely engaged in by ancient cultures. I am also convinced that this is at least one Spirit-charged way to bridge the growing chasm between human beings, our own deeper Selves, and Earth, on whose beloved body we all live, love, flourish, and die.

◆◆◆◆

Throughout this book, I explore whether a consciously lived life, actively grounded in daily, ritual acknowledgments of sacred connectedness to Nature, might bring about concrete changes in the value systems we abide by. I have always experienced Earth following the Gaia hypothesis of eco-philosopher David Abram when he speaks of Earth. His words mirror my own sentiments. "If the whole of this environment taken together with myself constitutes a coherent living Being endowed with faculties and powers far beyond those of its constituents parts, then everything I see, everything I hear is bringing me information regarding the internal state of another living entity."

In my relationship to and with Earth, I practice the discipline of bringing my Self into the equation with regard to any decision I might make that informs my connection to and relationship with her. Listening deeply and imaginatively to Earth is a discipline I have incorporated into my life. The result has been a lifetime of spiritual experiences framed within the heart of Nature that have allowed me to experience a profound sense of Self intimately related to the Divine in its manifest form as Earth in all her myriad beauties.

How do I describe this? I invite you to accept Jung's invitation to re-source your archaic self in order to re-inscribe into your lived reality the manifold inner being of Earth that long ago we envisioned and experienced as river gods, earth goddesses, thunder beings, lightning boys, tree spirits, and animal guides among a galaxy of other beings.

Let me paint a literary canvas illustrating this with a fragment of personal memory. As a small child, Earth, whom I named Blue Lady and understood to be God's truest emissary, educated, nurtured, and protected me through a period of irreversible wounding between the ages of eight and eleven years. During those years, it was she, who, in my tormented depths, sustained and gifted me in extraordinary ways. Although, in a beautiful irony, my solitary childhood was simultaneously rich with God-referenced visionary experiences in a world resplendent with wonder, mystery, creatures and other kinds of beings and magic.

More importantly, Earth in concert with the Divine, *responded* to my call as I did to hers. I would demand miracles as proof that God, in fact, did exist. And they would occur exactly as I wished but in *her* language. Stars would fall from the night skies on request and chosen creatures would appear on cue. Storms and rain would arrive when asked for, and rainbows, to show that I was still a beloved soul amid the deepening corruption of my prepubescent body.

It was Blue Lady who wrapped her arms around me with gentle breezes when I was too hurt to speak. When I had no idea what to do with my rage, she flung gale-force winds laced with thunder and lightning around my tiny body shivering outside in the garden. Then, the healing fragrance of dry, hot earth after a hard rain, commingled with orange blossom and jasmine that filled the golden air filled me with the promise of Grace and hope in a future I dared not see into. I am convinced, even today, this is the scent that pervades Heaven. It was Earth, colluding with the Divine, who was and still is my boon companion, my soul protector, my safe haven, and ultimately the true harbinger of my own redemption.

Jung describes a similar "divine rescuer" he experienced as a child and identified as God. "I often had the feeling," he shares, "that in all decisive matters I was alone with God and when I was 'there,' I was no longer alone, I was beyond time and belonged to the ages. These talks-experiences with the 'other' were my profoundest experiences, a bloody experience and also supreme ecstasy. Naturally, I could talk of this to no one. I remained alone with my thoughts. I played alone, daydreamed or walked in the woods alone and had a secret world of my own."

As an intelligence in her own right, when Earth as a necessarily effective agent of healing and authentic transformation is brought into the therapeutic equation, she rightfully becomes a coequal partner in the work of the soul. We are all walking wounded, and by extension so is she. So much of her beautiful body has been scarred and wasted by her increasingly toxic human children. Rivers are dying; creatures mutate; oceans store toxins enough to destroy all life as we know it; the sky is torn, and species essential to the health and wellbeing of us all are vanishing daily. Yet still her beauty, her unending, life-flowing, loving presence calls to us all if we are only willing to listen.

How will a small community of women experience ourselves, our beloved Earth as we attend to the call of our own individuating selves and to her call by participating in a Fire ritual? We gather to witness as each one of us ritually approaches Fire to heal wounds raw from feeding too much on memory, to rage against the feebleness of a hounded soul too weary to walk into the bright light of day. We circle up, tight and strong, to say, "Yes!" to change and "Yes!" to a newly destined future!

 JJJ

Extraordinary textual materials produced by the Fire sisters tell of their experiences preparing for and participating in the Fire ritual and form the heart of this book. From them we learn how critical it can be to human health and wellbeing for us to communicate profoundly, empathically, and lovingly with all beings in our natural world. At the same time, the journal entries and poems invite us in to witness the inner anguish we all experienced consciously or unconsciously as we took our selves wholeheartedly to Fire, to undertake the soul work involved in becoming whole and healthy women; in becoming whole and healthy Spirit-filled beings.

As one of the Fire sisters myself, I question the motivations behind including so much of my own personal story as an integral thread in the work. Is this a narcissistic move? Is this about an inflated sense of Self? Will this introduction of my own voice into the work somehow compromise its integrity? I turn to psychotherapist and author Maureen Murdock whose work on memoir and myth insists on the healing, teaching and centering function of writing down the stories of our lives, even if only fragmentarily.

From the start, it is important to admit that memoirs are a recollection of stories steeped in personal myths that are not necessarily reflected in our literal historical lives. In fact, although myths live in the realm of the creative imagination, they do serve a critically important function providing a way for us to make sense and meaning out of events and life experiences that simple hard facts are often not able to provide. We could describe myths as the foundational support of a psychic infrastructure made up of prominent archetypal blueprints and patterns around which we inform and shape ourselves, our experiences, our lives.

Writing about one's life in the form of a memoir is, like myth, a search for meaning and significance. Murdock tells us that "myth owes its persistence to its power to express or symbolize typical human emotions that have been experienced throughout successive generations [and to] its poignancy in portraying these enduring patterns of behavior or archetypal themes in an individual's life."

In fact, the texts produced by the Fire sisters are just that, memoirs describing a particular experience, a moment in life filled with rich and emotionally resonant poetic imagery, powerful affective symbols, and an intensity of focus and determination to grow and learn and change. They may also be seen as road maps that others can work from as they attempt to realize their own dreams and longings. Like myth, a memoir deals with human issues of ultimate concern. Murdock explains that, "myths explore themes such as alienation, abduction, betrayal, separation, death and rebirth. Rituals are mythic endeavors that call us to a deeper awareness of the act of living itself, our innermost struggles, our interior initiations into adolescence and midlife, the thresholds we cross from birth to life to death and back again." Because myths, including our own personal myths, transform over time and space according to the life lived, those of us who write down our stories can be viewed as the mythmakers of today. I hope the Fire sisters might, in some small measure, be viewed in this way as we gift you with our experiences and our ways with Fire.

I admit that not all individuals have the profoundly multivalent experiences in and of Earth that I have described. My hope is that what follows resonates joyfully with those who do, and for those who don't, it will open their hearts, minds, and spirits to the possibilities awaiting them. For the rest of it, this book describes the depth of my confidence in the efficacy of constant, ritual interaction with Earth as teacher, healer, and sacred conduit for encounter with the Divine. It tells of my love for her.

Transforming Self
in the Heart of Nature

MY OWN SELF'S passion play in relationship to God articulated in Nature runs in my veins like an ice-blue river rushing with the power of a snow melt in spring. Earth is alive, Self-aware, and actively engaged with all life forms that emerge from her body. We live, grow, make love, and die only to be reborn again into her green and wise ways. It is this foundational belief that shapes the nature and content of the soulful move that the Fire sisters make when we ask what a healing relationship with Earth and, by extension, with our own Selves, might look like, might feel like. And then, how do we recognize and open to Earth's own manifest interaction with and experience of us?

Each Fire sister writes with great passion and eloquence about her preparation, participation, and then incorporation of the Fire ritual into her life. Using the processes of creative imagination, meditation, and visioning during our four-week preparation phase, we ask Fire as Spirit *who* it is and *how* it wishes to be seen by each of us. We ask what it requires from us to engage in the ritual. Finally, we ask what *it* perceives to be our own greatest need for resolution and healing at this time. The resulting guidance then serves to inform our preparation and approach to Fire as therapist, teacher, healer, and spiritual guide.

It is this perspective, seeing Earth as the Divine embodied, that permits us to apprehend her voice such that we might converse with her as a daily, ritualized function. This is not a new concept. It is a lost concept. It is a forgotten fragment of the soul's code. It is no longer articulated in modern language precisely because the notion, for instance, that the wind speaks, that the hawk is the messenger of the Gods, and that rivers are lovers is considered simple-minded, an archaic cultural artifact. Our old-world translations of Earth's own natural language finds no relevance in a Western society culturally informed by the European Enlightenment, the Age of Reason and the scientific, industrial, and technological juggernauts of the postmodern age. Jung agrees: "Man feels himself isolated in the cosmos, because he is no longer involved in Nature and has lost his emotional 'unconscious identity' with natural phenomena. These have slowly lost their symbolic implications. Thunder is no longer the voice of an angry God, nor is lightning the avenging missile. No river contains a spirit. No tree is the life principle of a man, no snake the embodiment of wisdom, and no mountain cave the home of a great demon. No voices speak to man from stones, plants, and animals nor does he speak to them believing they can hear him. His contact with Nature has gone and with it has gone the profound emotional energy that this symbolic connection supplied."

In a microcosmic restorative effort, the Fire sisters attempt to identify and reclaim this ancient Nature-based language through our ritual engagement with the Divine in its elemental form as Fire. We invite it to voice its living presence in the prose and poetry that arises from the depths of our beings in response to our experience of preparing for and participating in the Fire rites. All the while listening deeply to the voice of Earth noting how we hear, see, intuit, and feel her presence.

As I prepare not only to facilitate but also to participate in the Fire rite, I grieve the increasing loss of the mythopoetic in the soul of our English language. I wonder if the Fire sisters need first to rediscover the particular voice and language forms through which our own truth as individuals striving to become Earth-centered human beings can be spoken.

In order to do this, we need to dream into being a new frame of reference that incorporates the ancient origins of our language. We need to liberate and revive the poetic beauties of a language depleted and diminished at precisely that level. We are too easily and too quickly acquiescing to the corporate drive for a new, globally referenced techno-language defined by utility, efficiency, and cost effectiveness.

Normal communication is being reduced to sound bites and limited by numbers and alphabets rather than whole words. "i lv u 2" or "r u there?" "☹!" This is the new, language currency sold as "hip" and "tight" to new generations of device-referenced and device-attached individuals. Certainly, we need to admit that this process is inevitable. After all, human history will move inexorably toward its own imperative while the species will transform in every aspect along its great sweeping arc, free-falling finally into its own enigmatic ending.

Nevertheless, there have always been those who work to safeguard fast-fading traditions. There are language preservationists who strive tirelessly to archive precious poetically inclined words that describe a deeper way of seeing complex beauties caught fast in the bittersweet paradox that is life.

When we forget the presence of soul in things, we begin to forget our own soul's presence. When we deprive ourselves of the means to preserve the soul of a thing—the fundamental purpose of language and speech—we deny language its own soul, a soul refracted exquisitely in each word dancing within the beautifully choreographed lines of each alphabet. We could even venture to say that language is itself an archetypal being, intelligent and Self-aware. After all, in its highest, idealized form, it has been identified variously in all human cultures as the Word, whose source is that aspect of the Divine called Creator. All things *resound* exultant in the created universe. Creation is a ceaseless surge. It is as an imperative, like ocean waves hugging the shore, or the promise of sunrise, or a snowmelt rushing toward its own conception—a rebirth.

So, we need to admit the presence of soul and of the Divine in language. Phenomenologist Gaston Bachelard reminds us it is only when we fully value language that we are able to interact with things to the degree that we may be able to hear them "speak." Language *creates* human consciousness, functioning through a dynamic of opening and enclosing like the delicate breathing of some exquisite deep-sea creature.

I imagine my first breath in this lifetime; it must have been the most sacred of moments, breathing life into myself every few seconds in order simply to remain here. I envision individual words breathing and dancing my life in whole sentences from the beginning of time, tripping the light fantastic with me across a thousand rainbows arcing across a whole universe of possibilities. Speaking words with beauty and power keeping the Sacred in mind requires loving the breath of life, loving the air that we breathe. It is an act of love to speak and sing, to laugh and shout, to moan and weep. At the same time, language as poetic expression opens and expands consciousness, leading to a profound engagement with the work of the soul, leading to illumination, liberation and higher consciousness.

For James Hillman, founder of archetypal psychology, words are containers. They are messengers. They may serve as hosts for archetypal presences, spirits, the Fates, or disaffected ghosts needing justice or closure. Yet, although they do in fact form the bedrock of conscious existence, words are becoming more and more alienated from the very things they serve to identify. Where do we go with this? Hillman explains: "How can anything of worth and soul be conveyed if archetypal significances are not carried in the depths of our words? Words, like angels, are powers that have invisible power over us. They are personal presences, which have whole mythologies, genders, genealogies, histories, and vogue and their own guarding, blaspheming, creating, and annihilating effects. For words are persons. Without the inherence of soul in words, speech would not move us; words would not provide forms for carrying our lives and giving sense to our deaths."

How is it to experience the *soul* of a word? How do we know when an archetype, spirit, or significant presence becomes suddenly present, clothed in a word or a phrase? How do we recognize a word containing the world or bearing a message from some sacred one? How do we *tend* to words that carry the contents of the soul between two people?

The Fire sisters attempt to answer these questions for themselves. We do this by welcoming the various forms in which our own experiences preparing for and then participating in the Fire ritual begin to language themselves in our journals and poetry. As we look to expand, enrich and deepen our lives through the intentional act of embracing the world, knowing that Earth will reciprocate, she begins to speak to us in signs and symbols pertinent to her own language forms.

＊＊＊

Why is a ritual approach to the process of Self-transformation important as an addition or alternative to standard, psychotherapeutic practices? Because standing on ceremony in the face of a particular thought process or complex situation allows the Self to reenact and experience the case scenario at hand from multidimensional perspectives.

Hillman tells us that the actual experience of ritual activity should never be bound literally by the strictly adhered to rules and regulations that often describe it. Ritual prescriptions by definition serve to *contain* the rite itself. They explain the purpose of the event. They describe the symbol objects and other paraphernalia used throughout the ritual. They explain the meaning and the significance of the actions involved. But, more importantly, rituals create a spiritual conduit for the participant to experience being guided by and, in some rare cases, fully consumed by the transcendent powers evoked in the ritual.

As a facilitator of rites of transition, I agree with Hillman that we cannot confine, predict, or shape the inner experience of the ritual participant. However, we do need to honor and adhere to the authentic structure of the rites with appropriately prescribed boundaries clearly in place. These culturally prescribed constraints permit the facilitator to maintain a profound engagement at varying levels with each participant throughout the duration of the ritual AND to provide a safe and sacred holding space for participants to freely access the presence and power of Spirit for healing and restoration.

Also important to acknowledge is that the overseer of the rites functions variously as a bridge being, an intermediary with the world of the Divine, a protector of the integrity of the ritual itself, and a guardian as participants surrender to the metaphysical dimensions of the soul work being done. Within the ritual setting, everything takes on deeper significances: intention, object, placement, movement, song, and prayer.

In this potent setting, the Fire sisters closely examine our own patterns of conditioned behavior and thinking. We work on ourselves to invent new models of behavior, to access the deepest levels of our creativity, to think constructively about our life challenges, our spiritual, emotional, and psychological needs. We invite Fire as Spirit to attend to our individual altars and to become intentionally active as guardian and guide in our preparations. We politely inform the *communities of being* that populate the inner landscapes of our own souls of our endeavor, inviting their positive contribution to our efforts. We watch for the appearance of transformational symbols, those that carry great significance, and mythically charged metaphors that may begin to story themselves up and out into our lived lives. We take note of significant synchronicities and even stranger twists of fate as the days move us toward the Fire rite. And, as the days turn into weeks, these preparations prove to be powerful agents of change for each of us.

A final level of preparation for the Fire ritual entails the creation of a sanctified, ritual space described by the world of symbol and myth. Then, during the rites themselves, we choreograph our verbal and nonverbal body language, body placement, and movement. Our eyes meet and meaning is made; prayers, chants, and mantras call in all beings for the purpose of praise and thanksgiving and for evoking the manifest presence of the Divine in our endeavors.

♪♪♪

Jung describes the world of symbol and myth and its particular wisdom traditions as "knowledge of a special sort; knowledge in eternity, usually without reference to the here and now, and not couched in language of the intellect." Instead, an anciently crafted language percolates up from the depths of the soul when a safe space to contain it is within reach: a place where words are liberated. Streaming forth, they are welcomed, celebrated and honored for their particular form of truth telling, for their poetic disregard of reason, and their depth of expression for the irrational. The Fire sisters' writings draw on this language of the soul to describe their experiences with Fire.

Mythopoesis in the human soul is seeded and then cultivated by what Jung calls the archaic mind or archaic self whose core function is to nourish the instinctive, intuitive, Spirit-referenced Self. Know that your archaic self is alive and well within, it is always accessible. It is, in fact, a critical aspect of human being and forms our spiritual nature at its most ancient core. More significantly, the archaic self, by definition and by nature, is in intimate relationship with Earth. This culturally configured relationship is expressed by symbolic forms, totemic figures, personal and universal mythologies, dreams, visions, and historical experience.

Let me explain this by way of indigenous wisdom traditions offered by Jungian analyst Marie-Louise von Franz's in her description of the Naskapi hunter of the Labrador Peninsula in Canada. In order to survive from day to day, this indigenous Eskimo unquestioningly trusts in his viscerally intimate relationship with Earth and in his intuitive understanding of her instructive communications. In this way, he obtains an extraordinary knowledge concerning wind and light, snow and spring, and the subtle scents of creatures roaming the vastness of his frozen world. He is ever alert to the patterning of new snow shrouding an unforgiving land, to the alluring geometry of snowdrifts glittering in the arctic night after an ice storm, and the particular degree of sharpness of the frozen edge of an early morning wind caressing his cheek. He also knows the variant meanings behind the subversive shadings and tenuous depths of layered light on a blindingly white escarpment that tells of approaching weather, that holds the key to survival for himself and his village.

The Naskapi hunter knows the nature of snow and ice from the depths of his archaic soul; he understands how to survive in it while celebrating the beauty and meaning of the blinding white puzzle that is his world. He and his Self are boon companions in the heroic sense of that term, bound with a vow of service to each other in life, in death, and beyond. For von Franz, the Naskapi hunter's soul is his inner companion whom he calls Mista'peo, meaning friend, an immortal being that lives in his heart and who will walk with him forever.

It is as clear as day to him that in his glacial world, Earth, his mother, must create as well as destroy in order to maintain life. In the same way, as simply one among many other animals roaming the ice-driven tundra, he must also take a life in order to live his own. He accepts that Earth can be an augur of hope, offer a safe haven and become a guarantor of life itself while in the next split second mark him for certain death.

It becomes imperative for him to intuitively "read" and "listen" to Earth's unending commentaries to all beloved creatures living on her body. He has no choice but to learn her language for it is his only means of survival, it is his only connection to her thoughts, moods, and patterns. As many tribal communities still do, the Naskapi hunter embraces, sustains, and sanctifies the culture-bearing mythologies that describe his own world in Spirit-filled terms. It is a world where basic physical survival is of paramount importance and impossible to accomplish without a deeply experienced connectedness with Earth as Sacred Mother. It is a world of wind and snow; of interminable spans of light and dark. Then, of fleeting visions of green earth shining under a sun-filled blue sky where birds flock and warm-blooded creatures roam the fragile, blooming landscape for just one moment until the snow triumphs once again. There is an eternal truth of great beauty in this for us all.

❦❦❦

There is also the notion of the circle of life, the medicine wheel, the mandala, and of eternal recurrence, that demands our attention. Like a labyrinth, the journey toward individuation or enlightenment has a spiraling configuration, with the Self at the center around which we ritually circumambulate ascending higher and higher. On this path, we learn our life lessons, opening to experiences that will change or mark us forever, grappling with unexpected challenges, or surviving crises until help arrives. Along the way, if we are blessed, we may be permitted to return "home" to rest, recuperate, and replenish our resources only to set out again on an even greater quest— our own Holy Grail.

When we embark on our individual inner journeys toward Self-discovery, toward enlightenment, toward our own sacred origin, we undertake one of the most dangerous courses in life. And those that survive along the way often point out their own personal saviors. For some, these "saving graces" may take form as angelic or other spiritual beings, or appear as ancestors. They may be steadfast relatives or friends. They may be experienced as an inner voice that guides in whispers, insights, and other particular certainties or like Moses on Mount Sinai, may be heard as the thundering voice of God. For others, these saviors may take the form of symbolic, totemic objects resonant with their own particular powers. They may be discovered in natural settings: sacred sites filled with the fragrance and mystery of the felt presence of the Divine: a grandmother rock, a grandfather tree, the spirit of a river, or the overarching protection of the spirit of a mountain. They may also appear as iconic figures in the communities that populate our dreams.

How are these boon companions experienced, and, perhaps more importantly, what is their role on the inner journey toward individuation? It is to accompany and to witness, to guide and to guard, and to protect the individuating Self from her own Shadow. You see, the Shadow encourages the urgings of misdirected outer and inner entities/self-aspects whose sole purpose is to distract, dissuade, and misdirect the adventuring soul toward at best incompletion and at worst failure.

As I have already mentioned, from the perspective of the soul-referenced Self, there lies within our beings an interior landscape peopled with communicating self-aspects replete with their own sense of individuality, purpose, and mission. And together, they comprise a dramatically alive inner world fully interactive and deeply engaged with the personal outer world. The work of the healthy individual is to know and maintain a constant balance between these entities who populate her inner world and who "feed" and function on the affects—the emotional fall out, of her life experiences. This fallout, like any kind of debris, settles and is absorbed into her ground of being like fine silt in the dire aftermath of a flash flood.

As our bodies are re-created every three months by the foods we consume, so our Self in all its aspects is re-created and nourished by the emotions, thoughts, and spiritual nutrients we feed it. Both physical sickness and soul sickness are the result of the toxicity contained in what we consume. In the same way, as the physical body is nourished by foods appropriate to it and poisoned by foods that are contaminated or are simply not for human consumption, so too the human *being* is either nourished or poisoned by the nature and kind of experiences that occur in our lives and by the ways we choose to deal with them. Do we feed ourselves joy, love, kindness, visions of beauty, honor, integrity, Self-respect and courage? Or, have we consciously or unconsciously set up an IV drip of constant sorrow, rage, guilt, anxiety, weakness, abandonment, fear, envy, greed, lust, and doubt?

So it is, that during a physical, emotional, or soul crisis, impassioned internal discussions take place. Discussions that, like lightning, are often charged with a storm of fear, confusion, disagreement, and contradicted information that make effective peace talks between the ego-personality, the rational mind, and the soul-referenced Self well nigh impossible. Yet, these discussions are imperative to the safety and wellbeing of the whole person.

As a reminder, the consequent actions or decisions negotiated during these inner confrontations between *all* the voices involved depend on whether they have correctly interpreted the particularity of the situation, its meaning, and its significance. Because these clarifications will provide the guidance and the tools the individual needs to create appropriate responses that will lead to positive and permanent change underscored by joy, passion and new depths of inspired wisdom.

The search for Self and the Divine, for healing and wholeness, for peace and reconciliation, for a life lived deeply and full of meaning is not an adventure that ordinary folk usually entertain. For those of us who walk this battle-strewn path, most have been more deeply wounded than blessed. Wounds that scar like shining stigmata, forming enigmatic hieroglyphs exquisitely chiseled into the depths of our beings.

Scars and blessings, these graces coil over the fragile tissue of a shining soul like ancient black and silver serpents beautifully encircling sacred white stones. Primeval and silent, we soul workers dig into the bedrock of our own beings until we catch the sweet scent of our own Divine origins streaming toward us like fragrant incense burning in some glorious heaven or in an even deeper twilight of the Gods. And it is here, in the depths of our own beings, that we pathfinders of the Spirit draw strength, support, and inspiration to forge onward in the constant company of Earth, the Divine, each in the company of our own boon companions and always, the ever-present Shadow who must be included, and above all, loved into the light.

᠉᠉᠉

In looking for deeply meaningful ways to reach out and touch Earth, we reach in and heal the Earth-referenced aspects of our own

Selves. In this way, we may make the necessary changes in our own lives in order to be more responsibly caring toward the natural world that nurtures and sustains us all.

How does one go about the task of reconciling psychologically or soulfully with Earth? How have others described Earth's nature and human nature? Is there a reflective move going on here? We humans often describe each other as being sweet natured and loving or having a stormy personality, or a cold temperament. We can be seen as having the noble heart of a lion or expressing the soaring spirit an eagle. We can be described as having the fiercely territorial and independent nature of a tiger or of being as timid as a mouse, of having a reptilian personality, or an evil, serpentine streak. There is great power in these symbolic images especially when we adopt and then systematically live them out as Self-descriptors.

We need to be cognizant and exceedingly careful of the symbolic or mythic images we clothe ourselves in because if we are not paying attention, *their* stories may override our own and *they* will live themselves *through* us. As Jung cautions us, the archetypes more often than not will hold us captive and transfigured if we let them, just like a spoiled child or an out of control puppy does.

How do these living symbols express themselves in each of us? Look at yourself in the mirror. Are you individualistic and career-centered, or communal and sharing in nature? Is your primary reference point in life ego-centered or soul-centered? What is the foundational emotion that drives your life energetically? Is it anger, resentment, fear, anxiety, competitiveness, inferiority, envy, love, kindness, fairness, or compassion? In fact, how does one's own nature influence the whole of one's being in relation to Nature? These are the questions the Fire sisters negotiate as we prepare for our participation in the Fire ritual.

Again, how do we embrace Nature? The Fire sisters are attempting to find out. We are consciously individuating women admitting our ongoing need for deeper levels of soul work, for increased connection with the Sacred in order to achieve integration within the very core of our beings. So, we take our yearnings, our dreams, our fears and failures, and our commitment to actively Self-evolve literally to the ground, to the Fire.

French historian Henri Corbin gifts us with his beautiful explanation of how the relationship of the human soul to Earth was viewed as sacred by the 5th century Persian prophet Zarathustra in his holy book the Zend Avesta. In this ancient text, Zarathustra personified Earth as an angelic or spirit form of the Divine in this world, and named her *Spendamart*, Earth-in-her-Angel.

Corbin reminds us that when we *meditate* Earth, we realize that it is not so much about the *essence* of things as it is about the *personhood* of things. We want to know not *what* Earth is, but *who* Earth is. We want to know *who* the natural elements are and to *whom* they correspond. When we do this, images as persons or other beings that correspond to or reflect our particular state of mind appear, whether literally or metaphorically. For instance, the god of thunder appears when we are roiling with rage or calling out for an injustice or injury to be avenged. The goddess of love appears when we are searching for an impossible love or wasting away from a broken heart. Messenger gods arrive when we cannot say the things that need saying or do the things that need doing. Rain gods send a deluge when we desperately need to be cleansed or to sprout new life from a drought-ridden existence.

Even more critical is the depth of meaning igniting the image and how intense that ignition is. Is the image simple or complex? Is it beautiful, horrific, frightening, or transcendent? Does it carry enough weight, enough volitional energy, to transform us? How much depth of soul moves in the heart of the image? How fully animated is it? How truthfully reflective? How intimately does *it* see into your very depths making it impossible not to respond? These are metaphysical inquiries that cannot be fully apprehended let alone answered by the rational mind. Instead, the soul searches for her answers through the creative or inspired imagination and by *experiencing* her embodied life profoundly.

Unrelated to any physical sensibility, the creative imagination functions directly as an organ of intuitive or inspired knowing. It is just as real and as vital to human survival as are the sense organs. This is the work of the soul occurring in a unique dimension of consciousness. A world that is at the same time inward and transcendent that we can think of as a storehouse of Spirit-sourced wisdom. It is a place where the Divine converses with the Self who in turn is gifted with graces and wisdom, forgiveness and compassion, and loved into a higher level of being. It is a radiant dimension where visions, revelations, and spiritual ecstasies occur.

In preparing to create the sacred space for the Fire rite, I will meditate Earth-in-her-Angel. I will also resource my own personal mythological archives to create a ritually prescribed sanctuary containing Fire not only as a natural element but also as a fragment of embodied Divinity. I will also create a threshold, in both the literal and archetypal sense, for the Fire sisters to move physically through into the ritual space, while simultaneously shifting into a soul-referenced state of being. Gazing into this otherworld, we will invite Earth-in-her-Angel to accompany us. In Corbin's words: "To come face to face with the Earth not as a conglomeration of physical facts but in the person of its Angel is essentially a psychic event which can take place neither in the world of impersonal abstract concepts nor on the plane of mere sensory data. The perception of the Earth Angel will come about in an *intermediate universe*. The Earth has to be perceived not by the senses, but through a primordial image that carries the features of a personal figure, and is experienced as so many personal presences."

Here, in this intermediate universe—the soul's core, changes in attitude, opinion, and approach to conducting the soul work necessary for inner transformation are facilitated by the creative imagination. According to Jungian analyst Jeffrey Raff, the creative imagination is the means through which intuitions, insights, visions, and revelations can occur, either directly or through inner dialogues with helping spirits or allies. In fact, the Fire sisters intentionally establish a relationship to and with Fire as a boon companion from the preparation stages to full participation in the Fire rite.

As we move closer to the time of the ritual, we experience ourselves moving into ever-deepening transformative states in our meditations, our journals, and poetry. Our dreaming, visioning selves are reaching farther into unconscious realms to reveal what we need to bring to the Fire.

It is extraordinary how the psychic energy released simply through our intentionality is constellating for each of us around a personal complex or complexes whose need for attention becomes immediate. It may be a complex of issues bound up in an unresolved aspect of a father-daughter relationship. We might be striving to override a chronic and long-standing failure complex. Maybe serious inner negotiations need to take place around a life yet unrealized. We may have to call on the powers of a true king to release ourselves from a complex structured around a profound delusion or disappointment that seems lodged, like Excalibur, in stone. These psychically energized complexes in turn attract and activate reflective archetypal communities that, like moths to a flame, appear in our lives in various guises sometimes beautiful, sometimes fearful.

Because the path to Self-knowledge is challenging and often dangerous, each Fire sister consciously identifies and invites the archetypal community who appear in her sphere of consciousness to tend to the complex or complexes that are beginning to make their way to the forefront on *her* behalf. At the same time, we are well aware that this invitation may, of necessity, lead to the reopening of dire wounds safely hidden long ago and that profoundly painful lessons are often the gifts that come with being willing to face the scald of old agonies.

The Fire sisters accept that new levels of humility and courage will be required as our hair and eyebrows are singed by the rising blue-tipped orange flames, as our fingers are scorched when we offer the Fire its ritual food, and as we place personal precious objects in its burning white heart. As women engaging ritually with Fire, we also know that we ourselves are Fire beings! We are formed, informed, and contoured from light particles as are all living beings, and as such, we are intimates of Fire.

Life flows like a great river moving unerringly toward its own origin. Lightning scores the sky with the hand of God. Fire sweeps across the landscape like a fury, changing the face of the land in its progress and, like the wind intent on its own metamorphosis, leaves, as its only mercy, ashen remains; an exquisite irony guaranteeing life in the heart of its own lament. The Fire, the ritual, the small community of women individuating on sacred ground invoke this cycle.

Each woman comes to the Fire bearing the gift of her own personal tragedy to feed the blue-red-gold flames. Each hopes that she, like the fragile yet invincible alchemical salamander, or the glowing phoenix dying into herself again and again, will rise from the ashes to live and grow into the power of her own promise. And, in that fiery embrace, will obtain a *cardiognosis*: a heart knowledge that depth psychologist Veronica Goodchild refers to. A particular kind of knowledge that "teaches us about the ways and wisdom of the heart, exposing us to beauty, and moving us toward action based in compassion." To take action based in compassion is to move out across Earth-in-her-Angel for the sake of love for it is in the radiant heart of reflective love that we transform.

CHAPTER TWO

Creating Ritual Space

IN HOLLISTER, CALIFORNIA there is a small reservation called Indian Canyon belonging to a small community who are descendants of the Mutsun Band of Coastanoan Indians. In the heart of Indian Canyon, inside the *Tupen Tah Ruk* or ceremonial arbor, four women will gather to prepare and participate in a Fire rite.

In my role as facilitator of this rite of transformation, I will first spiritually dedicate the ground that will serve as the ritual setting. Then, I will design the space to reflect a living mandala that in turn becomes a spiritually-charged vessel where profoundly transformative processes can be experienced within the prescribed ritual activity. I embed the site with symbolic objects and channel the presences they embody. I sing spirit-calling songs and place herbs and other sacrificial foods on directionally placed altars. Sacred entities may come to assist or simply to accompany me in my work. They will serve as guides, guardians, and boon companions.

The process of creating a sacred space for rites of transformation is informed in profound ways by my own orientations and practiced involvement with world cultural and religious traditions. In fact, as I describe the process, the depth and breadth of my experience in creating this sacred space, we will meander through time, visit other cultures and roam the world in no particular order, but that is how it works in the world of myth and archetype and Spirit. with me.

My formally stated intentions are welcomed by my own muses or spirit guides whom I experience as tangibly felt presences. They instruct me to mark out and design the ritual space in the prescribed circular form of a mandala, similar to the medicine wheel from the perspective of Native American spirituality.

I am guided to place carefully selected objects at altars situated in directionally oriented locations around the ceremonial arbor: East, South, West, and North. These are cherished objects charged with symbolic and mythological significance related to my personal experience and soul-connection with Earth, Divinity, and my own Self. Later, the Fire sisters will bring their own ritual objects and offerings to place on these same altars or on additional, personal altars they may have been guided to create during their on-site preparations for the ritual.

So, I do not prepare alone. Using my own ways with meditation, creative imagination, inner journeying, and visioning, I visit with and invite spirit beings and beloved deities to accompany me in my endeavor. Some are totemic beings representing the natural world. They walk with me in my dreams and accompany me in spirit in my waking life: , hawk, blue heron, salamander, hummingbird and dragon. Others are from worlds beyond who in this lifetime, in lifetimes already lived and those yet to come, minister to me and accompany me on my journeys.

Like a mirage shimmering through a veil of gold, they appear at the Eastern gates out of the ancient worlds of the Mediterranean, Persia, and India. From the turquoise heart of the Southern gates they dance toward me, some disguised in Christian garb, hiding their identities to all but those who know the still potent and ever-present spiritual realities of the indigenous cultures of the American Southwest and Central and South America. From the thundering Western gates, they rise and rise again tall and true on prancing ponies, keeping their ghostly distance, yet remaining in view, knowing that soon a great honoring of their spirits and ancient ways will take place. Then, from the snow-mantled Northern gates they stride brightly toward me with a fearless, shining certainty: great Norse spirits and deities carrying with them the traditions of the Vikings, the Saxons, and ancient Celts. The arbor here at Indian Canyon becomes a place where spirits abound. Here each Fire sister may safely enact her Fire rite receiving protected passage as she reaches out, at times tentatively, at times heroically, for her own healing, for a final return to her own truth, for redemption.

❧❧❧❧

Here is where the journeying involved in creating sacred space begins. It is about permitting one's Self to move beyond the constraints of reason, outside the limitations of linear thinking, and inviting a greater good to guide the experience. So, before continuing with the description of creating ritual space, I want to talk about the spirit of place.

Archaic and early societies, and now contemporary Earth-centered communities, establish sections or clearings of dedicated land that are marked out exclusively for rituals and otherwise sacred purposes. Anciently, these sacred groves, arbors, or temple clearings provided sacrosanct abodes for gods and goddesses and a myriad of other spirit beings who might take up residence in these holy environs when ritually petitioned by particular human communities.

In fact, Jung was particularly sensitive to the spirit of place and quite purposefully built Bollingen Tower, his home and spiritual refuge on the shores of Lake Geneva, on land that had formerly been the site of the ancient monastery of St. Gall. In fact, Jung had several of his most important transformational, paranormal experiences there.

Similarly, Indian Canyon provides spiritually dedicated ground for the Fire sisters to carry out our Fire rite. Certainly Earth in her entirety is sacred; yet there are places that seem to be uniquely imbued with an almost palpable energy, an indwelling presence that solicits special recognition and acknowledgement by anyone who approaches with respect. According to geologist Richard Ely and psychologist Anodea Judith, this energy may be measured in the form of concentrated geomagnetic currents that are known to occur specifically at certain sacred sites.

This indwelling spirit of place is often transcribed into the experience of sensitive people who describe the feeling as a heightened joy or a viscerally felt union with Nature as Spirit. For many, this connectedness transforms into a clear sense of individual purpose and personal commitment to making a contribution to positive change in the world on behalf of Earth. Others may be given much needed inner resources to make painful, yet ultimately beneficial, life-changing decisions.

From an aesthetic perspective, the geographical area containing the sacred site may be so spectacularly beautiful that one becomes literally enchanted and cannot help but be swept away in the deepest sense of that term. For transcendentalist and nature poet Ralph Waldo Emerson, beauty is an expression of the creative universe, and as such, the seeking, innovating soul is inexorably drawn to Nature to "feed" on sheer beauty in its purest and most affective form. "The beauty of nature," Emerson states, "re-forms itself in the mind, and not for barren contemplation, but for new creation."

Indian Canyon is one of these sacred spaces. It is hidden deep in the Gavilan mountain range and is well nigh impossible to find if one did not know the way. It was originally a hideaway for tribal chairperson Anne-Marie Sayers' ancestors, who escaped from slavery and confinement in the San Juan Bautista Mission in the early 1700s, remaining successfully hidden in the Canyon for several generations. Skeletal remains and village debris including mortars and pestles have been ritually reinterred inside the Canyon, itself undisturbed over the centuries. Halfway into the canyon is a small cultural center, while the rest of the land is dotted with traditional ceremonial sites. There is no electricity per se, only well water for personal use, a small creek, and a sacred waterfall whose healing waters have been used for centuries by indigenous people from all over California and beyond.

As you drive into Indian Canyon, you leave the modern world outside. You shed the 21st Century skin that holds you together just like the turquoise-bellied lizards that sunbathe on the rocks by the small creek. A sense of your archaic self appears at the threshold of your consciousness, ready to be lived into being once more. It is an ancient, eternal way of being, a sense of Self that takes your breath away.

Then you begin to breathe *prana*, a Sanskrit word meaning breath of life. It is a special kind of sacred breathing that Earth in her conscious wisdom makes available as an act of love to any creature that affirms her personhood. All other life forms, it seems, know this to be true. What might take a yoga or meditation devotee years to learn happens effortlessly for the Earth-being who mindlessly and joyfully simply says, "Yes!" while silently and safely opening to life.

In the Canyon, there is a certain kind of bright silence that pervades the land, rising like an illuminated white mist across the landscape of your own soul. Suddenly, you know yourself in a particular and truer way. Suddenly, you are moved by a sense of reality that is about being right here, right now!

This is not to deny the possibility of the same intensity of sacred connection occurring in New York City on Madison Avenue on a crowded Saturday afternoon. A sudden, instinctive downward glance, and there, in a black crack on a grimy sidewalk is a tiny, green, leafy being reaching bravely for the sun, struggling to make itself known in an unforgiving jungle of concrete even if just for a moment. And, just for that moment, a human stops to enjoy its shocking viridescence, glorifying Earth and the Creator for this sweet, unexpected, tenuous introduction. These meetings and greetings last a lifetime. I know, because that tiny green creature stopped to look at me in the same instant that I stopped to gaze at its wonder on Madison Avenue over three decades ago!

Meanwhile, here in Indian Canyon, there is a radiant vibrancy that bespeaks generations of ceremonial dancing, singing, storytelling, Fire rituals, sacred herbs, and prayers that still resonate in the shimmering air. Communities of tree people crowd along the creek side and clamber up the hillsides: coastal live oaks, madrones, and buckeye. There are bay laurels, cottonwoods, dogwoods, and bull pines, and along the creek, red willows nestle among the sycamores as do tule reeds and rushes.

Edging the wide trail that cuts through the Canyon, stinging nettles and poison-oak clusters caution the unaware while bracken, sword, woodwardia, maidenhair, and golden bat ferns sweep the enclosing hillsides. Along the canyon floor, herbs grow in profusion for the nourishment of the soul and the body alike: California sage, black sage, and mugwort, along with watercress, miner's lettuce, chickweed, and wild gooseberry.

In the early days, bears and elk roamed throughout the Canyon. Today, wild boar, wild turkeys, rabbits, and silver foxes still frequent the land. It is this tiny portion of Earth's beautiful body that provided everything for the small band of California Indians who took shelter and refuge centuries ago. Many families lived, prayed, danced, and died in this special place, and some remain as joyful ancestor spirits of the land. They gather closely and may be seen and felt when indigenous and other communities from around the world gather to conduct their rites and ceremonies.

So, the Fire sisters come to this special place bringing with us our own ancestral and cultural realities. As we open our hearts and minds to Earth here, she arrives in forms with signs and symbols that each Fire sister recognizes as her own.

For my part, great goddesses will not be left out of the introductions. Here is Artemis, the Sacred Woman of the Wilderness. Here is Earth Mother, Maka Ina, for the Lakota, and Tonantztin, for the Azteca. This is Chochmingwu, Corn Mother, for the Hopi. Here is the Freya, Viking goddess of love and war, and here is the great life bringer and destroyer, Shakti-Kali Ma, from the Hindukush. Here is the Virgin de Guadalupe, and here is Mother Mary. Here too, is Earth-in-her-Angel. You will get to know them.

Now, I must begin to clear the arbor and prepare a ritual space that will serve as the spiritually interactive field in which we Fire sisters will carry out our inner work in a safe and secure environment.

My companion, John, and I have already done most of the heavy physical labor. I am grateful that he responded to my plea for help to prepare the site for the Fire rite. As is often the case in land-based rites, hard physical labor comes first. Working the land ritually, as Jung has invited us to do in order to make our return to Nature, is also a holy act.

Before John and I begin our work, we waft ourselves with the smoke from burning white sage, cedar, and copal as a cleansing ritual. Using smoke from fragrant and sacred herbs or oils is a method for clarifying and spiritually dedicating individuals or places found in religious and spiritual traditions worldwide. We use traditional herbs used by tribal cultures in North and South America. They assist in establishing the prayerful, purified, and Spirit-filled state of being that is necessary to our work of creating sacred space. The specific cultural meanings and significance of these plants will be forthcoming.

We clear old brush, split and carry fire wood, clean and dig out the Fire pit. Under normal circumstances, I would have waited for the other Fire sisters to arrive and we would all have pitched in as part of the ritual activity itself. But, I am skirting what turns out to be a major, incoming weather system. Thunderheads are gathering with force overhead, crowding out a silver sky deep with portent and heavy with anticipated rains. Time to perform the Fire rite before this massive storm shouldering the Western skies hits will be precious, and the window of opportunity small. Before the sun rises, John and I work in an early morning drizzle in silent efficiency so that the ritual may begin as soon as the sisters arrive and, we hope, be concluded before the deluge of rain due to arrive late afternoon.

After we have cleared, raked, and made perfect the ground in the arbor, the next phase is to create a threshold or portal through which the ritual participants will step into the sacred site. I had dreamed the night before of the Fire sisters individually stepping across a threshold into the arbor. I saw us moving from one world into another. Once inside, we were there for the duration of the rites.

Engaging with Spirit often requires an absolute position. Earth herself is bound by the laws of her own Nature; natural laws that are incontrovertible and demand unquestioning obedience. In my dream, the very act of our stepping across the threshold into the ritual site was momentous, its gestural quality signifying archetypal meaning far beyond the act itself. Each Fire sister carried an attitudinal stance that Aztecs anciently and presently refer to in Nahuatl as *me-shika tiyawi,* meaning: "Go on your way looking forward, without a backward glance." In other words, once the die has been cast, the gauntlet thrown, or the intention set, we must move out toward the goal, with determination, trust and absolute certainty because there is no turning back. A promise is a promise. A vow must be kept.

The threshold, both as a literal and metaphorical space, is where decisive actions or experiences occur that may stall or move us forward on our life's trajectory and, by extension, our Self-development. Threshold is a Teutonic word rich in symbolism, significance, and affect. It speaks of greetings and farewells, of constant comings and goings. As an architectural device, a threshold is literally a timber sill or a stone platform placed as an entranceway to or an exit from a building or a hall. It is often the strongest point in a building's design and thus the safest place to be when, for example, Earth decides to quake. It is a pragmatic, spatial, and mythic word. It is an archetype.

There are many cultural traditions that require participants to engage in "crossing rituals" before entering or exiting a designated sacred space. Muslims perform prescribed ablutions that they may be made clean, and women respectfully cover their heads and faces before entering a mosque. Roman Catholics dip their fingers in holy water and make the sign of the cross over their faces and hearts as they enter the church.

Among various California Indian tribes, mugwort or bay laurel leaves are considered powerful plants with attendant spirits that protect sacred sites and hearth and home from malignant spirits or witchcraft targeted toward individuals, families, or the entire community. Bunches of mugwort are packed around lintels that secure doorways, along windowsills and other openings, and around the boundaries of communal areas. This powerful plant protects individuals, families and the tribe from a variety of harmful contingencies.

The word threshold also contains the word thresh. Threshing is a process of shaking, beating with a flail, or mechanically manipulating grains in order to separate or release them from their husks so they can be cleaned, polished, and made ready for consumption. How many times have we been buffeted about by the Fates and "threshed" or "thrashed" in an experience that shakes us to the core? While every attempt to escape or deny the given moment is thwarted. Severe wounding can occur to a person at the threshold of any given situation, circumstance, experience, or journey. In fact, we may arrive at the starting gate, as it were, already battered and bruised. Jesus of Nazareth's Stations of the Cross on the way to Golgotha and his crucifixion is a particularly dramatic example of a threshold experience that has served devout Christians as a powerful metaphor for the eternally suffering soul's struggle toward salvation.

Psychologically, a threshold also indicates our physical, emotional, or psychological capacity to undergo either great joy or great suffering. Strangely enough, it is possible to measure and calculate whether we have a lower or higher limit of endurance when it comes to dealing with stress. For instance, with physical or emotional pain, if we are not able to bear the slightest infliction we have a low pain threshold. Someone who is able to withstand what, in normal circumstances, would be considered extreme, even unable pain has a high pain threshold.

A threshold may also serve metaphorically as a guidepost to the border regions of our inner world or the depths of our being. It can mark the beginning or ending of an experience or undertaking. Crossing the threshold takes great courage and faith for one may not know what is on the other side or what dark and measured possibilities lie in wait, hidden and watching.

There are numerous threshold gods, but for me, it is the Egyptian-Roman god Janus who appears to me in a dream before the Fire ritual and serves as my guide to creating the threshold for the sacred site. I choose to use the present tense when I refer to deities or other forms of spirit presences because I experience them simultaneously in their eternality and immediacy.

Marie-Louise von Franz discusses Janus in his ancient Egyptian form when he was named Aker and was imaged as twin lions sitting back to back, each leaning against a sun disc that was held between them. For me, this image and his later, double-faced Roman portrait are conjoined across historical time. As a unitary being, Janus-Aker simultaneously faces the past and the future while holding firmly onto the present represented by the sun disc. The sun as element and symbolizing the Creator aspect of the Divine is eternally dying and resurrecting in order to maintain the cycle of life, always looking toward the promise of a new dawning while gifting *his* reflection to a dark moon whose magnetic grip on Earth's watery depths is absolute. Together they ensure life itself.

Janus-Aker serves archetypically as Usher and Guardian for souls traveling between worlds. The act of crossing the threshold can also be said to represent an inner dimension of being through which the soul-referenced Self bravely travels back and forth between spiritual and earthly realms, from inner to outer and back again, where she suffers, undergoes symbolic death and rebirth, and receives graces and blessings both in her embodied and spirit form. Marie Louise von Franz tells us, "Janus-Aker also represents a kind of sacred space that contains the images of everything which exists. He watches over them and has them in his arms." In my dream, Janus-Aker accepts the invitation I send out into the universe for a sacred one to come to my aid to bless, guard, and protect the Fire rite, the Fire sisters, and the sacred space in which we will conduct our soul work.

There, in my dream, on either side of the West entrance to the arbor, stand twinned six-foot wooden poles, tall and straight, representing Janus' two-directional orientation. They form the threshold through which the Fire sisters enter the arbor. In the dream, the twin poles have streams of ribbons tied to them that fall down their length in the seven colors sacred to many ancient world cultures: red, the color of the East, spring, eagle, and Earth; yellow, the color of the South, summer, deer, coyote, and air; black, the color of the West, autumn, thunder, lightning, and water; white, the color of winter, buffalo, owl, and Fire; green is Earth, blue is sky and Creator; purple stands for the Great Mystery or all that we can never know. In my dream, I sense that each of the Fire sisters is uniquely experiencing moving across the threshold. For me, it is like slipping through an invisible force field that feels like an electric shock and then suddenly stepping forth fully free onto holy ground.

The arbor in Indian Canyon is cut into a small, tree-studded hillside and is surrounded by ancient oaks. As I begin to meditate the placement of the ritual objects I have brought, it is entirely appropriate that I leave John to clean and dress the twin poles with the ribbons. He sees them as his spirit brothers and will approach them likewise as a brother-in-spirit whose task is to prepare the poles as "bodies" for the dual spirits of Janus-Aker to reside in for the duration of the Fire rite. He quietly strips the bark off the two tall willow staffs, then purifies and dedicates them with smoke from burning sage, rosemary, and sweet grass. As he prays in honor of each sacred color while tying the lengths of ribbon to the poles, I remember that the name John is anciently derived from the Latin name Janus and the even earlier related Greek name Ionnes. The connection is incidental and beautiful.

When the twin guardian poles are ready, he prepares the holes in the ground with a dedication prayer adding to them a pinch of cedar in remembrance of the now extinct sacred cedars of the ancient cultures of Egypt, Persia, and Rome, then cornmeal—food for the gods. He securely plants our twinned god into the ground. Then, blesses the whole site beginning at the East direction and moving in a clockwise direction with a glowing sage wand. Meanwhile, I place the bowl in which the sacred herbs are being burned on the East side of the threshold, keeping it lit throughout the day so the fragrant smoke of cedar, sage, copal and other mixed herbs waft constantly throughout the small arbor, securing its sacred designation.

Cedar has been burned anciently in rituals all over the world.

During the Fire ritual, we will burn it to protect us from harmful energies that may appear as deprecating thoughts, emotions, and intentions negatively sourced from within our own selves. Remember, contrary spirits abound whenever and wherever something good, brave, and soul-directed is going on. The sweet, pungent smoke from burning white sage maintains the purity, clarity, and beauty of the Fire rite as well as of the inner state of the participants. Copal, a sacred resin used in Mexican and South American indigenous ritual, releases a fresh, piney scent that is said to attract the ancestors, spirit elders, spirit teachers, and other benevolent beings. The Fire sisters will be bathed in these fragrances all during the day's ritual activities. My choice in using traditional Native American herbs for this land-based part of the ritual activities has to do with respecting the fact that we are conducting the Fire rite on traditional indigenous ceremonial ground.

Inside the arbor, just off center and standing to the East, an elderly California oak rises. She has presided over the Canyon and everything that happens there for generations. As a very young oak, her trunk split into two beautiful limbs gracefully raising themselves upward toward the sky, reaching for the warmth and light of the sun as if opening to a lover. In between her limbs, at the base of the tree, a soft, dark-green, mossy round offers itself as an altar for the encircling twelve sticks of burning incense with which I gently inoculate her tender yielding.

Incense is burned throughout the day in the deep hollow of the oak. The scent-filled arbor beckons the spirit-world and Earth herself. As the air becomes richly fragrant, I lay a polished rainbow abalone shell filled with crystals, turquoise, coral, and obsidian inside the circle of incense wands. The oak is now an altar dedicated to the Divine Feminine—Earth-in-her-Angel. *She* has been *activated*. She has appeared to me as a wise elder, Grandmother Oak, and in this form, her wisdom will guide and sustain me as facilitator throughout the rite.

I place exquisite figurines and other symbolic images around the base of the oak that depict, among other things, sacred women and deities that are precious to me. These are spiritual companions who are active within my Self, not only in regard to the work I am to do this day, but they have been guiding, teaching, and inspiring me throughout the weeks of preparation. It is important that I tell their stories and introduce them to you because they form a core component of my own inner community. They populate the inner landscapes of my soul, coming and going at will. They are my boon companions accompanying me in the deepest sense of that word. They are witnesses to the journey I take toward my Self, toward the Divine and toward my own origin. My own origin: some call it Heaven, or Nirvana; I simply call it "going home." This is how it is, being caught up in and by the Divine when one is fully engaged in a spiritual endeavor such as this Fire ritual. We travel in spirit, we fall into deep reveries, and we surrender to metaphysical forces that draw us into other worlds and times, into alternate states of being.

ﮋﮋﮋﮌ

Here is La Virgen de Guadalupe. She is revered by the indigenous communities of Mexico simultaneously as the Mother of Christ and as the Azteca goddess, Tonantzin, or Earth Mother, who kneaded humans into existence from sanctified cornmeal and breathed the breath of life into them. Today, as in the days of the Conquistador, devotees light candles and burn copal incense in their small chapels and outdoor altars to honor her simultaneously as Creatrix, as ancient Earth Spirit, and as the Virgin Mary! This is a superb popular syncretism worthy only of the Catholic Church.

During seasonal celebrations, indigenous country folk garland the combined altars to La Virgen de Guadalupe and Tonantzin with flowers and traditional indigenous foods as ancient as the ground itself: red, white, blue, and yellow corn, the colors of the sacred four directions; then melons; brightly polished dried beans; and squash. There are traditional elders from indigenous Mexican communities who insist even today that it is Tonantzin, disguised as la Virgin de Guadalupe, who saved the spiritual traditions of the Aztecan culture and, by extension, of the tribal peoples of the New World. According to current, indigenous interpretation of extant 16th century historical texts describing the Spanish invasion of Mexico and subsequent holocaust of the indigenous peoples, it is actually Tonantzin who appears as the Virgin Mary to the Aztec peasant Juan Diego on a hill just outside Guadalupe, a hill now graced with the re-created Aztec temple of Teotihuacan. According to the Catholic interpretation, in this vision, the Virgin Mary urges Juan Diego to instruct his people to embrace the true faith of the conquerors.

In the cryptic version, however, Tonantzin instructs Juan Diego to tell her people to safeguard their own spiritual teachings, rites, and wisdom traditions by hiding them deep inside the ceremonial bedrock of the usurping religion until a time when it would be safe to reveal them again. According to this interpretation, indigenous spiritual elders then knowingly encouraged Spanish missionaries to build chapels and cathedrals over well-known, ancient temples and sacred sites in order that the spirits and powers of their own sacred ways would seep through the walls, altars, and Catholic rituals and thus continue albeit in foreign finery. For instance, following the Spanish Conquest in the early 16th century, the temple to Tonantzin at Tepeyac outside Mexico City was destroyed. In its place a chapel dedicated to the Virgin Mary was raised. We know according to observations made by the Spanish priests at the time that newly converted indigenous people traveled long distances to worship there, and insisted on addressing the image of the Virgin Mary as Tonantzin.

Embracing la Virgin de Guadalupe and bringing her into my life in ritually directed ways continues to be a healing process. She guides me in the ways of constancy and love, compassion, and understanding. She has also taught me how to "play the game" as a smart woman who exists in a world that continues to revolve around the worst elements of religiously endorsed patriarchy. She shows me how to remain soul-intact through it all while begging the lie. She teaches seeking women about the power of the mask, the persona, about when to hide and when to reveal our true Selves. She teaches us to safeguard the bitter and the sweet secrets while treasuring the wisdoms they hold. She tells us when the moment is right to unfurl our true colors and to brook no obstacle. She reminds us when the time is right to spin a useful tale, and in the telling to lovingly "tend" to the offending one.

Because her formidable spirit and tender presence need to be with me during the Fire ritual, I place a beautiful Oaxacan hand-carved image of la Virgin de Guadalupe at the base of Grandmother Oak encircling her with pink roses and votive candles. Next to her, I stand a white alabaster sculpture of the Roman Catholic image of the young Jewess we call the Virgin Mary tenderly clasping her first-born son. With her strong, gentle presence, I am also honoring one of the Fire sisters, a devotee of the Mother of Christ and of the Magdalene. These two images side by side represent again a twin image of the same mysterious female being, representing at core the Great Mother, and the bearer of Divinity.

Continuing to prepare the ritual site, I am increasingly aware that the archetype of the twinned or dual-aspected being is being constellated for me as a powerfully personal complex. My thought process and creative work is taking its own turn. I am feeling emotions that seem to be mirroring the threatening storm clouds gathering overhead and wonder if the Fire sisters are being moved in the same way.

☽☽☽☾

Then, placing beside the Virgin a small, flat rock upon which an image of Blue Corn Maiden is painted, I smile for the Hopi and Pueblo peoples of New Mexico, for whom she is a happiness carrier, a peacemaker, and peacekeeper. She is a bridge being. She nourishes her people with corn that is produced on Earth's body. But it is the spirit of the blue corn in particular that imbues and informs their souls of her Beauty-Way translated from the world of Spirit into their everyday lives.

Blue Corn Maiden maintains the balance between the powerful and incendiary summer and winter Kachinas whom she loves and honors equally. A Kachina is a familial spirit being who represents each facet of the created world for the family, the community, and the pueblo. There are thunder and wind Kachinas. The spirits of insects, deer, eagles, s, and buffalo are embodied by Kachinas as are the spirits of revered ancestors and mythological heroes. I say familial because Kachinas are themselves represented as having kinship relations with each other as lovers, married couples, parents and grandparents, children, siblings, etc.

It is important to note that Kachinas are not worshipped. Each is viewed as a powerful spirit being who, if given veneration and respect, may use their particular powers for human good, for example, bringing rainfall, healing, fertility, or protection. I live my life under the gentle tutelage of Blue Corn Woman. I wear her sacred name given to me by a pueblo elder and relative by adoption. She is my namesake, my guardian, and guide, and she has now joined me for the Fire rite. She will stand by the Fire sisters bringing her gift of peace and balance as we undertake our soul work today.

꜊꜊꜊

Now it is time to girdle Grandmother Oak with several large shining abalone shells. Abalone shells reflect the light and gift of rainbows. Rainbows are a calligraphic sign of the mercy, compassion, and constancy of Divine love. They are sacred and spell joy. Encircling the altar at the base of the great oak, these abalone shells testify to my abiding love and affinity with Earth when, at the beginning of time, she appeared as White Painted Shell Woman to the Apache tribes of the American Southwest.

In fact, it is from her body that the Apache emerged into the created world. It is a Beauty-Way story. In the beginning, when the first light of the first day shone crimson and gold upon creation, kneeling in the rush of a sparkling river, White Painted Shell Woman, in prayer and supplication, raised her arms to embrace the morning the palms of her hands facing the golden light. In that moment, his gaze falling upon her beautiful rainbow body, Usen or Life Giver, in his form as the sun, fell head over heels in love. Gathering her up in an azure veil of sky, a storm of love was made from which a great fall of sacred beings, the Mountain Spirits, tasked to care for the Apache, descended into the world. Soon after, White Painted Shell Woman gave birth to the first of the Apache, the twin brothers, Child of Water and Slayer of Monsters who traveled the world to make it ready for those that would follow. How peoples across the world story their own origins and how we individually tell of our own beginnings, is a mysterious and sacred ritual that must remain inviolable.

As an ageless spirit, White Painted Shell Woman is an inextricable aspect of creation itself, renewing herself beautifully in an ever-recurring cycle from youth to old age and back again to youth. In this way, she remains always young, graceful, vital, strong, and able to carry out her sacred destiny for as long as the world turns. The abalone shell I wear on my body, represents an abiding reverence for what she signifies. I "wear" her so that my own body being may hold within itself the radiance of *her* rainbow body. Yes, as a human I am mortal. But, like her, I am also eternal, existing in spirit and other forms through endless cycles of Self-evolution.

I now cultivate a soul-relationship with certain Abalone spirits who reside at the ocean's edge along the California coastline skirting the Pacific from Monterey Bay to Big Sur. Over the years, they have taught me songs, shared the sacred and medicinal uses of their bodies, and of their rainbow dwellings: exquisitely beautiful shells that for them *are* the created universe.

My first teaching from these spirit-Elders was not to put Fire to the abalone shells as so many do when they burn sacred plants or incense in them. You see, the abalone both in sentient and spirit form offers sage teachings about light in relationship to the rainbow and, by extension, to the Divine. This humble sea creature lives its sentient life camouflaged in coral encrusted crevices, clinging for dear life to rocks and cliffs in the ocean depths, fighting to hold on against the constant pressure of swift cold currents. Human hunters brave cold and dangerous deeps to gather abalone, whose treasure and gift to the world is first and foremost nourishment, and then, even more spectacularly, its humble home, which, when opened toward the sun, becomes a shimmering jewel, a presentiment of Paradise.

The rainbow blazing out from the abalone shell is a signifier of the light that the Self yearns for. And so this "painted" shell asks to be cleaned, polished, and then beheld with the eyes of a seer, the eyes of a mystic, the undisturbed gaze of a seeker of deeper wisdoms. There are worlds of light and teachings to be found within the brilliance shining out from the rainbow heart of the abalone shell, and especially here among the tribes of the American Southwest, there is nothing more precious to be had or to be gifted with. I am reminded of Jung's words: "The longing for light is the longing for consciousness. The moment in which light comes is God. That moment brings redemption, release." They are true jewels of light in both senses, these abalone shells. I need their rainbow secret with me this day, and the ocean rush they emanate.

A stream of significant images, sensory perceptions, intuitive personal responses, and instinctive reactions has me welcoming the felt presence of archetypes and of other spirit communities who are now crossing the threshold, intentionally situating themselves around the arbor as I work. Making themselves known to me in their own unique ways, each will take an active role in the transformative dimensions of our experiences during the Fire ritual. The Fire sisters will get to know these spirit presences more intimately as we move toward the rites themselves.

﹥﹥﹥

The altar at the base of Grandmother Oak is expanding and deepening in power and presence. Now, nestled among the abalone shells and resting against the trunk just before she splits into two skyward thrusts is a blue-green clay tablet. It depicts in quiet beauty a Cretan Earth-goddess who was first celebrated and honored by the Ancient Minoans on Crete 5,000 years ago. She is a Bronze Age goddess whose image was found on clay tablets, pottery, and coins at the

Palace of Knossos and in numbers of royal and sacred sites scattered throughout the island. She wears the dress of a Minoan queen, her outstretched arms holding serpents revered both as fertility symbols and as symbolic of her role as protector of the Cretan world. On her crown is seated a dove of peace, her own sacred bird. We do not know her name but I know by implication that she has many. Anciently configured in this precious and timeless image cast in clay and situated at the root of Grandmother Oak, I smile at her. She sees the meaning in my eyes.

For me, this Minoan beauty represents the Divine Feminine. She is a sacred trinity composed of the Greek goddess Artemis, the Cretan goddess Eleyetheria, and the Mesopotamian goddess Ishtar who are the same deity, named, identified, and described in cultural particularities by their own peoples. All three are here.

Anamnesis, Jung's word for experiences of past lives, is key to my connection with this archetypal triad. Either they appear unexpectedly, suddenly activating deep within my Self, or they fall from the heavens making themselves known reflectively in my external reality. In certain instances they set about *re-transcribing* my existence into my conscious awareness on their own terms especially when I need to negotiate a particular moment that requires the investment of my whole being across time and space.

I think of Jung's description of his travels through Kenya and Uganda in 1925-1926 and of how he notes a profound sense of knowing himself as a *continuity* throughout existence. I love that term! On the trip from Nairobi to the game preserves of the Athi Plains, he admits to experiencing a *déjà vu* at the deepest level, "I had the feeling that I had already experienced this moment and that I had always known this world, which was separated from me only by distance in time. It was as if I were at this moment returning to the land of my youth, as if I knew it and the people, as if I knew the 'solitary dark hunter' of that land for 5000 years. The 'feeling-tone' of this experience accompanied me throughout my whole journey through 'savage' Africa." Here, in Indian Canyon, gazing into the heart of the image of this wondrous Minoan Earth Queen, I am transported in spirit back to my beloved island of Crete. In fact, it was on Crete, as a young woman on a pilgrimage to sacred places around the world, that I first encountered my beloved goddess triad.

Crete is a magical and sacred isle embraced jealously by Homer's "wine dark" and fierce Aegean Sea. Straddled by snowcapped mountains, sliced through and through by deeply cut gorges, graced with river-nourished fertile valleys, and shadowed by the darker side of heaven, it is the birthplace of the highest gods and goddesses of the Greek Pantheon including the great Zeus and the twin deities Apollo and Artemis.

Here then, as a young woman not yet twenty one years, this trinitarian goddess came to meet me in visions and dreams, initiating me into her/their mysteries and, as they do with all their devotees, fashioning me into a fourth to complete their sacred quadrant, bringing me into their sacred circle. They continue to beautifully shape and inform my life.

That particular journey took me from the Greek Isles, across the Middle East to India, and then to Indonesia, where fate spun a mystery and brought me to the United States. Here, my inner life and soul journey shifted toward the transcendental teachings and practices of the Upanishads and the Buddha, Sufism, later grounding itself quite literally in Native American and other indigenous spiritual traditions. For almost three decades now, my sacred connections with my European, Nordic, Middle Eastern, and Asian roots have been safely secreted away in the treasure troves of my own Self.

Then, a year ago, I was guided through dreams and visions to retreat to Crete for healing and rejuvenation, to reclaim my relationship with each goddess and to embrace them once again into my own present tense. You see, as a result of my intensive commitment and profound participation in indigenous spiritual practices, I had held them in suspended animation in my inner world, unconsciously preventing them from penetrating my conscious mind or informing my Self-awareness as they had been used to doing.

But, I discover, they still have important work to do on my behalf. They also have special need of me, in the mysterious ways that gods and goddesses do when it comes to human devotees and their "bridging" function whereby deities and other spirit beings move between incorporeal and corporeal worlds. "If you dream of an archetype in a human form," Marie Louise von Franz tells us, "that means that you could, to some extent, incarnate it. It could manifest in you, and could express itself through you." This is not new. The Divine in all its myriad forms has been speaking to and teaching us from the beginning of human time through the agency of our great messenger spirits/angels; signs, symbols, dreams and synchronicities; prophets, prophetesses, seers, and philosophers; poets and artists. Embracing this way of thinking calls for what Jung calls a mythical consciousness, a particular form of understanding.

James Hillman puts it this way, "Just as we do not create our dreams, but they happen to us, so we do not invent the persons of myth and religion; they, too, happen to us. The persons present themselves as existing prior to any effort of ours to personify them." By way of an illustration of what is meant by "mythical consciousness," where the boundaries of time and space disappear, I will describe my recent winter pilgrimage to Crete knowing that this is what is at play for me here in the arbor at Indian Canyon. I am falling into a reverie. Experience deepens becoming boundless. Come with me.

I am in the airport in Athens, ill from an exhaustion that has driven me to the point of despair. I have never known this kind of "running on empty," my body is on "red alert." Board the plane to Crete, I know as sure as life itself that it is literally *this* beloved island that has "called" me to rest and to heal from a world-weariness that threatens to injure me beyond repair.

The moment the small propeller plane rises into the shining air and begins to move across the azure depths of the Aegean toward the setting sun, whispers of Homer's Iliad and Sappho's poetry begin to recite themselves in my mind, and I realize instantly that there is more afoot and yet to be revealed. Electrified with a generative energy that I immediately recognize as my soul on a mission, I breathe, go inward, and feel the whole of myself—truthfully. I look toward Crete as we begin our descent, gazing at the charcoal thunderheads in the Western sky that have formed themselves into a silver-lined cloud-temple worthy of the great Zeus himself, replete with columns and a stairway leading to the temple threshold. Here are gods and goddesses standing witness to my arrival on this sacred island.

I watch my beloved sun god, Phoebus Apollo, blazing his way through the center of these cumulus temple columns flinging shafts of red-gold radiating out over the altostratus steps leading up to the sky-temple entrance. I welcome his embrace. Is this my own interpretation of what I am seeing among the silvered clouds? No. Am I the only one who has asked for a personalized greeting from the island and her Graces upon my arrival? Possibly. Every passenger however, Greek and foreigner alike, is exclaiming at the sight using religious-inspirational terms to describe these temple festivities taking place in a glorious god-filled sky. All those on one side of the tiny plane step over to the other, asking passengers if they could look through the small windows so they too could enjoy the wind, cloud, and sky-divine spectacular. The pilot orders them back to their seats as the small aircraft begins to dangerously tip. The plane is having serious trouble balancing itself. My heart is racing, my mind knows its rightful place, my soul soaring. Extraordinary! It would be the perfect Homeric moment for me to simply disappear, lost forever in the Aegean. Sheer poetry!

But I want to focus here on the reunion with my beloved trinitarian goddess in her forms as Eleyetheria and Ishtar yes, but primarily as Artemis. For, while on Crete, as part of my restored bond with them and a renewed promise to incorporate them fully into my life once again, I invited them to guide and work with me around the upcoming Fire rite and with the Fire sisters.

Also deeply meaningful here is my reunion with the totemic bear spirit from that hallowed isle, connected as it is with both Artemis and Virgin Mary. Crete is a luminous island where bears once roamed wild and where women ritually worked with their totemic spirits carrying, interpreting, and administering the wisdom traditions of bear to the communities—herein lies my heart's delight and my soul satisfaction.

Interestingly, during this retreat on Crete, I also experience visions where I am brought into an unforeseen and joyful reunion with a very particular kind of inner wildness that has to do with the Viking strain in my blood. Suddenly, old Nordic words, invocations, and the evocative and resounding images they embody, stream into my mind, heart, and soul like fresh, sweet water suddenly released by rapidly melting snows, enlivening me in ways I remember as an unbridled young woman. They now welcome me "home."

Historically, the Vikings did sail the Mediterranean in the 10th century their ravenous eyes firmly focused on Greece and her strategically situated islands. And so, over the days and weeks, I find myself caught up in the electric atmosphere of ancient memories arriving like an invading force: ephemeral scents, deep-running emotions, exotic sensations, blood and secrets, unbroken vows, love and death, a gauntlet thrown, and sweetest of all, no shame, nor fear, or holding back in being a strong woman in the face of strong men. All this and more flows back into my consciousness like a banshee fighting a windstorm on her way to Valhalla.

That Viking streak shot straight out of my past, landing in my present along with the Norse Gods Odin, Thor, and Freyr along with his twin sister, my beloved Freya. With them appears in silent, sacred splendor a vision of the axis mundi or World Tree, Yggdrasil, a bridge to the beginning and to the end of all the worlds. When a call from the heart of a human soul resounds in the universe, great beings will appear when and where they will.

And so, here on Crete, in the small coastal town of Hania, and into the eighth day of rest, sleep, and walking by the Aegean, I dream one morning of three women in white robes dancing in circles. They dance holding hands but two hold out their hands to an invisible fourth as if waiting for her to appear at any minute. That fourth, in herself, is also an incorporated trinitarian being: me, my Self, and I.

Joyfully responding to the invitation to join their sacred choreography, I enter their circle, dancing the vision.

Blossoming in the shining air as it layers itself around the exquisite body of this island, shimmering like so many beautifully transparent veils on the living ruins of ancient enchantments both radiant and terrible, I am deeply moved by the spirit of place. Moved to travel across Crete to pay my personal respects to small temple ruins; out of the way, unkempt, and decidedly pagan sites where I am instructed in dreams and visions to perform specific rites. Thankfully, these neglected and hardly visited holy places are wondrously responsive to my presence. Earth speaks. Flocks of white doves suddenly alight close by, attentively watching my sacred rites at the temple of Asklepios, the Greco-Roman god of healing.

In the early hours of a dawning day, a pearlescent moon silvers a tender farewell as Phoebus Apollo arrives on the horizon in a glory of gold. Venus, Ishtar's own sacred planet, flashes blue, white, and purple at dawn and at twilight with a brighter intensity. Silver foxes shyly appear, hawks and eagles wheel overhead in the luminous air, while along the rocky paths leading to small shrines, wild goats congregate as church bells ring insistently, desperate not to be forgotten in the splendor of it all.

ノノノ

Then, at sunrise one morning, I awake to the whisper of Artemis inviting me to visit her at the place of her birth, the cave of *Arkoudiotissa,* she-bear. This is the earliest ceremonial site dedicated to Artemis that we have on historical record, dated 2600 BCE.

I respond, as I always do when Spirit calls, immediately.

Traveling for an hour or so, I finally arrive at a tiny Greek Orthodox shrine cut into a great cliff face beside the entrance to Artemis' bear cave. It is dedicated to the Virgin Mother. Entering out of a greater respect for all sacred sites, I find a cheap, faded print of the Virgin, dust-encrusted, with mold creeping toward the center of the image like the scent of death. The glass in the frame is cracked, burned-out candles lie strewn about on an earthen floor desecrated further with broken beer bottles, cigarette butts, and Coca Cola cans. It is to this sad, disheveled, disrespected, and neglected shrine that a few hardy Christian pilgrims and tourists arrive. What a terrific disappointment! In this fundamentally chauvinistic world of Greek Orthodox Christianity ruled with a religious iron fist by the Patriarchs, it is indeed a sad testament that, for the most part, it seems only chapels dedicated to male saints are well tended by the locals, their overtly declared dedication to the Virgin Mary notwithstanding.

Fortunately for me, I am traveling out of season and few visit this out of the way Artemis sanctuary. In fact, visitors and locals are generally discouraged from entering the dark maw of the huge cavern. It is deep, very dark, and, as one moves into its heart, the silence is resounding. *This* is one of the greatest of divine gifts: finding oneself *entirely* alone in a sacred place thousands of years old with ground uneven and dangerously slippery, having been polished by the feet of countless devotees over millennia. A threshold.

Treading carefully, fully alert, I move into a stark emptiness countered by the immense fullness of a *felt presence* that warmly drenches the space curling like a lioness in heat deep inside my own belly. And then, suddenly, I am gripped by cold. A chill hand reaching out from the beginning of time through the cave walls strokes my skin. Ice seeps into my bones. Shadows grow longer. I move down and down again surrendering to the draw of the darkness now almost impenetrable, all the while fervently thanking the stars above for the gift of modern technology I hold in my hand: a flashlight.

In the center of the cave rises a stalagmite about twelve feet high that, depending on one's approach, may appear as a raised on her hind legs, an ancient, hooded crone, or a beautiful, discrete woman hidden behind a heavy veil. Experiencing the enigmatic force emanating from this mysterious tri-faceted female figure sculpted by the forces of Nature in white calcite leaves me shaken, trembling.

I approach with reverence, falling to my knees instinctively, and with bowed head, raise my hands in supplication. I have, after all, come to tend to the goddess as she has instructed. Although the air is charged and heavy, it is not oppressive and the ground, like skin, is strangely silken, soft, and smooth. Suddenly, I feel a loving touch on my forehead above my eyes. I feel a whispered breath on my eyelids inviting me to open my eyes. I sense *her* beside me as I would my best friend, in quiet comfort, with full understanding of each other, in love with each other's good and trusted company.

As I meditate on this figure, I begin to "hear" her breathe, to feel her "flesh" radiating life and, like an iron filing to a magnet, I am irresistibly drawn to place my body against hers clinging for many moments to her gracefully curved torso, yet knowing it would be dangerous to linger too close for too long. A strange surge of exhilaration captivates me, it is an ignition and, knowing how to fly, my soul imagines preparing to leave my body then and there, with a fervent salute, and a rousing fare-thee-well.

Then, *she* rises up in stone leaning over, gazing deeply into a large, raised naturally formed cistern replenished over millennia by constantly condensing water falling from the roof of the cavern. Healing waters. There are shallow stairs that one can climb to reach the water carved by numberless footsteps into the left side of her body. Climbing to the broad lip of the cistern caressing her smooth and strangely warm body with trembling fingers, I lay out my ritual offerings; olive oil, honeyed milk, rosemary boughs, and small abalone shells brought from the shores of the Pacific.

Tears spring to my eyes while I light twelve votive candles that reflect multiply through the depths of the cistern. I have come home. There is nowhere else I need to be. I want to spend the rest of my life in this bear cave. It is a good time to die and it will be a good death. The kind of death I pray for—a great story (in the epic sense) for my descendants to tell and embellish as time goes on.

I now lean deeply into her body for support as I feel my heartbeat slowing down. My breath is slipping away somewhere far behind me. Then I hear her voice whisper an enchantment, "Sweet one, know that I accompany you as you accompany me, it was always so; do you not recall our times together, my heart with your heart? Then remember me well in these ways. I have remembered you, my beloved. Listen to me! I have remembered you."

Jung says that, enchantment is the most ancient form of "medicine," and I recall how he describes his mother in classical Artemisian terms, "By day, she was a loving mother but at night she was uncanny, like a seer who is at the same time a strange animal like a priestess in a 's cave, archaic as truth and nature. At these moments, she was the embodiment of the "natural mind," which says absolutely straight and ruthless things, a mind which springs from natural sources, it wells up from the earth like a natural spring and brings with it the peculiar wisdom of Nature."

I lose track of the time spent conversing with *my* Artemis inside, and at the same time, far beyond that cavern. Much of the experience cannot be said because this is a level of soul work that demands isolation and calls for surrender to the mysteries involved and must remain unspoken. It is a particular kind of Self transformative process that Marie Louise von Franz describes as, "a real secret, for as soon as you touch the uniqueness of the process, or of the individual, it cannot be talked about anymore. There is the 'I am you and you are me,' in it, and that is the element which cannot be told. That is the *unio mystica* [mystical union]. But it is a real mystery, a mystical experience, one which therefore can never be [fully] imparted or shared with another person."

The sacred one I have come to serve this day appears by my side in all her three aspects. As I begin to consider where I really am and begin to absorb the wider dimensions of the experience, I can say in all clarity that innumerable lives were also sacrificially taken in this ceremonial site as spirit gifts and soul food for the goddess. The walls pulsate, embedded as they are, with uncountable silent promises, and lives given and taken over the eons.

It is also true that in her Eleyetheria aspect, Artemis safely midwifed birthing women and their infants into this darkly warm and humid gestational setting. I resonate deeply with the vision of the sweetness, purity, and grace of tiny new lives being brought forth out of the wombs of women into the uterine cave of a goddess, and then into the bright light of the life-giving sun, her own twin Phoebus Apollo.

I remembered the years when I myself had been a lay midwife throughout the years of the homebirth movement in the 1970s and 1980s. Now here, in this sacred cave, Artemis in her Eleyetheria aspect shifts the focus of my gift from midwifing the vaginal birth of a new soul into this world toward midwifing the seeking soul toward her own Self, toward her own sacred origin. This translates later in and around the Fire ritual, where it becomes my responsibility to create a safe "birthing" environment for the Fire sisters and myself. Where I must carefully monitor the birthing process, being prepared at all times to safely "catch" if necessary each of our newly born selves.

Meanwhile, here, Artemis draws me down ever more deeply into her dark radiance, turning and bearing me into her own wilderness. Yes, I know that if I want to safely retrace my steps back out into sunlight, there is a line I cannot cross. And, it is only at the gentle urging of her own wise Eleyetheria aspect that she finally gives way guiding me into the cherished arms of my ancient Sumerian divine, Ishtar, who will accompany me out of the Artemisian depths and back into my life. As the morning and evening star, it is Ishtar who has shone her twinned reality on me all my life, cautioning me when necessary, as a flickering flame does, to keep conscious and alert. We must remember that Fire, whether in the soul or in the world, must never be allowed to die.

I love Ishtar. She is bewildering and by nature, contradicted. As a peacekeeping warrior, she is fiercely gentle, as a righteous judge, she is merciless. She is a lover of ordered chaos and journeys into the light as easily as she sojourns contentedly in the darkness. In Ishtar, the opposites unite, polarities dance circles around the sun, and paradox is the poetry of her devotees, her own holy fools. The heavens tremble at her approach while her beauty breaks the most intransigent heart.

Her tenderness is unbearable and her compassion, like a newborn's grip on life. Do not mess with her. She is like a Viking warrior queen gone berserk, not necessarily a bad thing.

In her Artemis aspect she is the fearless huntress, her prey yielding at every twist and turn of an unending trail. She is unstoppable. Yes, and with her at my side, I am always able to go on, always able to somehow find the willingness to live. It is *her* vitality of spirit that has carried me safely through these past few years of running on empty. And, in *that* discussion, in *that* bear cave whose palpitating walls seem to be inscribed with the history of my whole existence, my life here and now has been re-gifted to me with resources fully replenished, all engines ignited and fully operational.

I emerge from the bear cave with the fabric of my Self, my world, and my destiny rethreaded and rewoven even more deeply into the story of these three sacred ones. And I am not alone. They emerge with me, and accompany me still, in the golden-blue light of my spirit, in the cerulean red and cobalt blue of my own blood stream, and in the lightness of my footprint. Walking back up the steep, rocky trail to the rented car, I speculate on how powerful it would be if there were a present-day ceremonial of Artemis as huntress, protector of the wilderness and she-bear goddess, *and* the Virgin Mother of Christ. In this way, I imagine a glorious, pagan-Christic worship that would invite all primordial gods and goddesses *and* God the Father, God the Son and God the Holy Spirit to the great hallowing. Yes!

To my great delight, as I read Peter Duerr's book, *Dreamtime*, on the flight home to California, I discover that February 2nd is the veneration day of the *Panagia Arcoudiatissa*: the Virgin Mary of the Bear! It is celebrated in small localities everywhere on Crete. Now, I am happy and at peace. I love a good contradiction, not to mention hypocrisy that I can sink my teeth into!

So, archetypes do roam free, blessing and cursing in turn depending on the human complex they are tending to and, of course, their mood. As metaphysical principles, they are always elusive, but as Hillman assures us, it's only when we are able to recognize them in personified form that "they become now recognizable as persons, each with their own styles of consciousness." As divinities, they "present themselves each as a guiding spirit with ethical positions, instinctual reactions, modes of thought and speech, and claims upon feeling."

Artemis, Eleyetheria, and Ishtar, all aspects of the Great Goddess, live for me as they do for each one of their devotees and for the world itself. This is both a joyous and frightening fact. From a Jungian perspective, the alchemical power of Artemis' bear-cave is fully operational for those who are willing to surrender to it. It is a place of purification, catharsis, birthing, dying, and transformation. As Jung insists, "whenever we touch Nature we become cleansed."

꠸꠸꠸

Let us return now to Indian Canyon, back to the arbor, and to the work of preparing the site for the upcoming Fire rite. As I continue to prepare the land and the ritual setting, I am aware of the necessity to provide a space that is both inspiring in design and beauty that will serve as an authentic alchemical container in which necessary transformation is possible for a willing soul. Once intentionally dedicated, this kind of sacred space, by its very nature, becomes inhabited by invited presences, and also by unexpected and uninvited invisible guests, who, once perceived, will need close and careful tending to throughout the rites. Believe me, there *are* mischief-makers who inhabit the spirit world and our own souls.

My intention is to create the ritual setting in such a way that the physical and the spiritual conjoin, where both worlds interface. I begin by asking Grandmother Oak to bless and dedicate my role and responsibilities during the day's work. Moving into my own state of receptivity to Spirit, I ask who wishes to speak through me at the Fire rite and what they wish to say.

It is common in the world of Spirit that questions are answered indirectly or in ways seemingly unrelated to the inquiry. And so, in response to my invitation, I am gifted with the following vision:

It is a bright, colorful day. I begin a journey that leads me to a beautiful meadow in which stands a Tree, beckoning as if it recognizes me and has been waiting. I recognize it as my own Tree of Life. The Tree instructs me as a teacher or guide would. During the preparation process leading to the Fire rite, I am to open to my own life process. I am to open to my Self as Tree and to look deeply into my own lineage. In the vision, Tree pulls me down to my knees, to its base, and I begin to dig with my bare hands, pulling at its roots. It seems an impossible task, but I am assured that there will be roots that will yield, as did Excalibur to Arthur.

I continue to dig and pull. Tree confirms that these roots are for me to consume and will be sweet, nourishing, rich. I begin to reach deeper and deeper into the ground, listening as Tree speaks of signs and directions and of consequential meetings that are to take place in my future.

Suddenly, I am walking inside the roots, which become a network of tunnels leading to numerous destinations. I ask where they lead to, and I am told that events have already been organized for me. In some mysterious way, it is known that I am on my way. I ask what kind of events are planned and Tree talks of wedding feasts and agreements, tokens being exchanged, promises to be made and kept, which will confound at first but which will bare precious fruit in times to come.

Ethnographer Lewis Hyde speaks of a special kind of gift that is soul-sourced and therefore elicits a soul-response. He personifies the ever-journeying gift as if the gift itself is a pilgrim and the journey of exchange it embarks on a pilgrimage. On its pilgrimage "the moving gift," which can be of either practical value or a spiritual offering, as in the case of my vision, will forge new relationships and protect the sacred underpinnings of a particular circumstance, situation, or endeavor as in the Fire ritual.

I will return a portion of Tree's gift to the Fire sisters in a ritual telling of the vision, giving it freely so that it can undergo its own metamorphosis and fulfill its own ultimate destiny in their retelling of it. It is a joy to "water" Grandmother Oak with my gift of grateful tears that fall onto her body.

An authentic, Spirit-sourced gift has nutritional qualities whether in the literal sense of foodstuffs or in an emotional or soulful sense. And so, from an Earth-centered perspective, we need to consistently return the gift in various forms to the gift-giver. You see, sharing is a defining quality of the human spirit, but only if it is carefully culti- vated and constantly tended to. As an example, Hyde describes this cycle of reciprocity in gift giving as it takes place around food among the Maoris of New Zealand. Concerning ceremonial functions he tells us, "A portion of the ceremonial food is ritually partaken of by the priests who then take the remainder of the food back to the forest to gift it back to the spirits who reside there with a prayer that future and continued sustenance continue to be provided by the forest and the spirits who dwell there in the form of all the life surrounding." The meaning and significance of the gesture is everything. Life cycles.

Now it is time to prepare the directional orientation of the ritual setting. I envision the Fire sisters arriving at the arbor and crossing the threshold into a living mandala resonant with archetypal and spiritual significance. A mandala, by definition, is sacred space. Mandalas de- pict a universe of symbolically charged images embedded in multi- dimensional patterns describing beautifully the ordered chaos of the universe and of the human soul. Classical mandalic designs are con- figured as quaternities or multiples of four. They are depicted in cul- turally specific artwork, sacred architecture, or designed as a shrine or ritual, sacred space. They can also represent a state of mind. Can you imagine a mandalic state of mind?

According to Jungian analyst Jolande Jacobi, the mandala sym- bolizes the primordial or original order of the soul. She tells us that Jung discussed the human soul as being founded on the alchemical principle of four. This is the power of the *quadratura circuli*, with the five representing the quintessence or the central mystery of things.

She continues, "Both the production of mandalas and meditative immersion in them can awaken or express this 'original order' that is potentially present in every soul."

We can say then that mandalas are mirror images of the human soul on its journey toward Self-knowledge, towards wholeness of being. Jung places ultimate value on the image of the mandala as the primary archetype for the process of individuation. He applauds its usefulness as a metaphor for the lived experience of the multidimensional Self as it constantly negotiates the inscrutable, perplexing daily challenges of life without losing track of its spiritual destiny.

We all have to deal with success, betrayal, failure, progression and stagnation, procreation and sterility. We all face oppression, disappointment, and humiliation, sometimes on a daily basis. We all will see and know illness, aging, and death.

Still, some of us are born to run with an imperative for life that streams like a lightning strike through the blood and the bone and into the deoxyribonucleic acidic depths—the DNA factor of our beings. An urgent passion compels us to search for precious ephemerals like truth, authenticity, beauty, compassion, understanding, joy, grace, love, God, and the ultimate meaning of it all. We dance life in a mandalic pattern, an ongoing process of formation and transformation, birth and death, mirroring inexplicably the whole eternal process of creation itself.

For Jung, mandalas are also cryptograms that speak a secret language pointing to the hidden workings of the soul. He says, "In them I saw my whole being actively at work and through them I acquired a living conception of the self." He goes on to describe the dynamic of the mandalic journey in the following terms, "I saw that all the paths I had been following, all steps taken, led back to a single central point. The mandala is the center, it is the exponent of all paths, the path to the center, the path to individuation."

Symbols like the mandala also play an essential role in maintaining healthy correspondences between the conscious and unconscious. It is crucial to understand the significance of symbols that appear or are placed in any field of endeavor because they provide a transfer of meaning that may bridge or unite opposing positions.

"Knowledge of the symbols is indispensable," Jung tells us, "for it is in them that the union of conscious and unconscious contents is consummated. Out of this union emerge new situations and new conscious attitudes." This is what I hope the presence of the powerful, symbolic figures I am placing in the arbor will elicit in the Fire sister's experiences during the day's ritual activities.

Fire is to be the *fifth* in the quadrant equation. It will represent the quintessence, the Self, centered in the mandalic configuration of four altars that I create on the perimeter of the arbor in respect to the cardinal directions.

In the North, I place a large bronze statue of the Shiva Nataraj. This is the dancing Shiva, confined within a cosmic mandala, itself aflame with the Fire of Divine love. In Hinduism, Brahma, Vishnu, and Shiva constitute the Supreme Being as a trinity. Brahma represents a distant, creative force whose Word results in creation, while Vishnu oversees the universal principles of truth, beauty, justice, love, compassion, and ultimate wisdom.

Shiva meanwhile, is fully engaged in overseeing the cycle of life, the circularity of constant movement, eternal recurrence: birth and death, Earth's seasons, and the precise workings of both the physical and spirit-charged dimensions of creation. For human beings, Shiva maintains the fragile balance between good and evil, illness and health, and the volatility of human emotions. Shiva is intimately involved with Earth.

Like Janus-Aker, Shiva is a dual god. He is an androgyny. He is a polarity: a bridge-being running back and forth at the speed of light between all opposites. He is a transcendent function. In his female, He is Shakti, the Divine Feminine who manifests as various goddesses at one and the same time. These goddesses are among the most revered and feared of female deities in the Hindu pantheon: Durga, the warrior-peacemaker; Kali, the Great Mother, and protector and destroyer; and Shiva's hauntingly beautiful and loyal consort Parvati, the ideal of perfected Hindu womanhood. The Nataraj Shiva shows the god dancing the universe eternally into being, for if the dance stops, even for a fraction of a moment, the universe as we know it, will disappear. I hope that the Fire sisters will resonate with this dancing image as we dance inside the arbor around the Fire and the Sacred Oak. I place a yellow stone at the base of the Nataraj, symbolizing the Light of Life itself, and a small bowl of fruit with sweetened rice milk as a traditional thanksgiving offering.

And now to create a Ganesha altar to the West; Ganesha is the beloved son of the twinned androgyny Shiva-Shakti. A fabulous elephant god, he is a splendid illustration of what occurs when polarities are willingly united in mutual love and understanding as in Shiva making love to his own Shakti in the form of his great consort, the exquisite goddess Parvati. In Jungian terms, this is the *animus* in perfect union with its *anima,* in my own terms, my female-identified self at one and at peace with my male-identified self.

Then there is Ganesha, the wondrous translation of the two united into a perfect third. Conceived by divine parents who represent, oversee, and are the embodiment of the universe in its ordered chaos, half man, half elephant, and born a most gracious god, Ganesha invites us to approach him with a light heart bearing gifts that must be beautiful and delicious. He is a deity who loves love. He loves women, and children. He is tender with the aged and infirm. He celebrates Earth's abundance and offers a bountiful life for his devotees. He is a wonderful host, and hospitality is a sacred art for him. He is a mediator and a peacemaker. He teaches us to compromise, to appease willingly when possible, and to adapt rather than to resist. He invites us to share successes and resources with family, community, and, above all, knowing the volatile nature of his great mother in her form as Kali, give back to Earth her due rewards.

Ganesha is here for and with me as "co-host." I thank him for honoring us with his sacred presence. In fact, I need him to guide me, to help me host the Fire and the gathering community of beings, both visible and invisible.

A beautiful Javanese Buddha carved out of wood the color of pale gold graces the South direction in quiet humility as does the sparkling purple quartz and the food offering placed beside him. The Buddha and his teachings, in particular, Zen Buddhism, which is the mystical child born of the union of Mahayana Buddhism and Chinese Taoism, presents a way for us to live into and through to the other side of things. This simple wooden carving invites us to be, like the bodhisattva disciples of the Buddha, compassionately attentive and committed-in-love to living recurrent lifetimes in this material world until all life forms are saved from the ties that bind us to this world. The Buddha teaches us in practice to disengage the Self from all attachments in this realm of existence. We must selflessly strive to go beyond all traditions, all ritual, all rational knowledge, and all history. He invites us instead to live in the fullness and perceived truth of the moment, fully engaged from the point of view of the ego, the physical body, and the reasoning mind while the Self's position remains correctly detached.

With the Buddha seated in full lotus along the central axis that runs through the circular Fire hearth, through the heart of the Sacred Oak and beyond, I feel the lines of radial energy begin to pulsate.

Finally, to the North, behind the Grandmother Oak, I create an altar to honor all indigenous tribal cultures, to honor the ancient ones, and the archaic world. I place a large petroglyph sculpture carved out of metal on an altar stone. It depicts a powerful shamanic figure with antlers on his head, large circular rings hanging from his ears, and lightning strikes cut down his chest. Here is where the Fire sisters will invoke the ancient ancestors and spirits of Indian Canyon to come join us and bless our Fire ritual and to watch over our soul work.

The next stage of preparation entails digging out and preparing the fire pit. John and I do this with prayers and lay offerings of fresh cedar boughs, white sage, tobacco, corn meal, sweet grass, beads of copal, fresh rosemary, honey, and thyme deep in the fire pit. The Fire will not be built or lit until the Fire sisters arrive to add their own offerings and prayers to the fire pit, itself an altar.

After the fire pit is made ready, I set up tables covered in lovely Guatemalan weavings on which I place ritual instruments: drums, rattles, flutes, clapper sticks, and bells. Hand-carved bowls are put out filled with sacred foods: sweetened saffron rice, herbs, resins, milk, honey, and olive oil. Herbs and other sacred plants are placed carefully in traditionally woven baskets to "feed" and "gift" Fire throughout the day's ritual activities.

At last, all is done. John and I survey the whole site. Without us noticing, in this deep canyon, it has suddenly and very quietly become enchanted.

THREE

The Fire Ritual

FIRE SISTERS, LUNA, Kit, Spring, and myself Ismana are here to participate in the Fire ritual. This small circle of four women have come to holy ground to re-collect, renew, and rebirth aspects of ourselves yet to be revealed.

With John having been responsible for creating the threshold, it becomes appropriate for him to welcome and bless each Fire sister with the purifying and calming smoke from the burning sage as she enters the arbor. We form an intimate circle just inside the threshold with him. We thank him for supporting us and the soul-work we are about to embark on this day. And, we know that during the day we will be reminded of his presence as we carry out our Fire rites in a sacred site whose breathtaking beauty is due, for the most part, to his hard physical labor and spiritual support. We will also remember him as we pass by the rainbow-ribboned twin poles representing Janus-Aker that stand strong and straight, solid and secure, guardians of the Threshold. We acknowledge our gratitude for his balancing and loving energy. It represents for us what we each have been seeking for in our lives for a long time, the right kind of communion with men who deeply appreciate, value, and honor women's ways in all their incomprehensible mystery.

During the various phases of the ritual, the preparation, enactment, and the closing ceremonies, we Fire sisters know ourselves as equals. We understand that it is the integrity, commitment, and conviction we each bring to the ritual that will result in its efficacy and authentic transformative impact.

We also understand that, during the rites, we may move into a trance or an otherwise altered state of being. But, let's be careful here. You see, it is the intimacy that is created between each other based on a *necessary trust* that establishes the "safety net" for the entranced soul to express herself.

I feel a surge of energy flash through me like a lightning strike. A generator has been switched on somewhere inside me too deep to reach, and my soul is on the move. Enchantment clings to the shimmering air overhung with heavy cloudbanks like the kiss of a rainbow dreaming.

A golden eagle circles above the tree line, his bright cry echoing throughout the canyon. Eagle is the universal, archetypal symbol for messenger. In the indigenous world of the Americas, he is the one with the ability to transmit prayers and supplications to the Great Spirit and bring back messages, guidance, and signs to the people. His cry is also a call to prayerful attention, much like a Muslim muezzin's mesmeric call to prayer.

Two ruby throated hummingbirds spark brilliantly, flashing to and fro around the rainbow staffs while a white butterfly hovers intently above us. The Grandmothers are here. This is what the presence of butterflies signify in some traditions.

A restless wind springs up. Oak leaves spiral in the air, raining a carpet of gold onto the circle of ground in the arbor. This is how Earth initiates a conversation with us. It is her language. Earth-in-her-Angel has joined us inviting her Earth-daughters to put rational thinking aside, and to give way to our creative, instinctual, and intuitively apprehending selves.

Together, silently, we acknowledge this joining with her. We can see it in each other's eyes, in our body movements, in the tone of our voices, and in the closeness of *all* proximities here in this sacred place. It is this kind of magical thinking that produces and cultivates *mana*, the receptive spiritual energy that electrically refuels or recharges the Self. It is an archetypal state of mind.

Instinct and archetype are, in fact, two aspects of the same thing. But, even more importantly for our soul-work during the Fire ritual, we need to make the connection between our instinctive responses and the presence of the archetypes in order that we might become conscious of what within us or outside of us has become constellated in the particular moment. As an example, I encourage us all to invite our communities-in-spirit, totems, guides, ancestors, and other sacred ones, to join us in our endeavor this day.

Standing by Grandmother Oak, I call the Fire sisters around me to share with them my sense of what ritual space is and the importance of us all moving into the formality of a ceremonial stance or attitude before we begin. I talk about my own ideas around the process of individuation and the search for our authentic selves. I describe the kind of soul-informed consciousness I hope we will all carry with us throughout the day and how that kind of consciousness cannot help but be interlocked with our awareness of Earth and all natural beings.

Sitting in a half circle by the Sacred Oak, the altar of the Divine Feminine at our feet, I talk about our need to bridge states of separation within ourselves, and with Earth. I suggest that in order to do this it is necessary to develop what I call peripheral consciousness that when operational, becomes a part of one's everyday sense of things. Peripheral consciousness is a state of conscious reverence. It is a mythical sensibility. It is a sacramental understanding of living amidst and within the living body of an intelligent and Self-aware Earth, who is both a personal and transpersonal being in her own right, actively in relationship with all creatures who source her for life and in turn ensure her own continuity.

Cultivating peripheral consciousness involves simple connective disciplines that have far-reaching consequences for us as Earth-referenced beings. What are these simple disciplines? Consciously acknowledging hawks perched on telephone poles, geese migrating, lupines carpeting green hills, or gunmetal thunderheads gathering along a silver horizon. Blessing the liberated spirit of every creature on the side of the road killed by traffic or electric wires. Voicing aloud or silently unlimited praises and thanksgiving for every kind of natural beauty that graces your vision and stuns your senses.

Remember to name these encounters. Naming things is a simple discipline itself. Keep the poetics of the instance always in mind because it's in the poetry that the deepening of the moment occurs, that the memory and the image are captured. Peripheral consciousness calls for a reawakening of the erotic soul: a soul enraptured with love for the Divine. It calls for adopting a new perspective, an addition of new values, and admitting Earth-in-her-Angel into one's daily life in both her extraordinary and mundane dimensions.

Hillman talks about this in terms of establishing an intimate intercourse with Earth by cultivating a sense of *notitia:* a deep affirmation of Earth's living presence. This affirmation requires an activated peripheral consciousness. It entails actively taking note of Earth's virtue and relevance and cultivating a heart-felt empathy for all Earth beings.

It is when God enters into the emotional equation, and the soul in love with Love takes the reins. It is where the Self stands on ceremony in the face of Earth's radiant glory, while steeped in her own dark mysteries. It is acknowledging a deep and sensual appreciation of the tastes, textures, colors, shapes, sounds, and scents of her Nature. We must give thanks for life—life lived here and now.

As the words continue to spill quietly into the surrounding incandescent air, all of us fall into a sweet reverie. We breathe in the light. I invite us to adopt this attitude of deep, soul-referenced observation. I ask that we consciously notice significant moments, occurrences, or synchronicities in this sacred environment and within ourselves and name them. You see, words create the container or the body for the soul of that which has been named so that it may live and function according to the vicissitudes of its own moment.

I talk about peripheral consciousness functioning in an alchemical field, a field that is by nature transformative. It is a profoundly aware state of being that is referenced both by Earth-in-her-Angel, on whose beloved body we walk, and by the reflective inner world of things: that inner universe where the transforming Self encounters the Divine and where either raptures or measured torments take place. A true metamorphosis is often caught up in the context of an anguished event dyed in the luminous splendor of a consciously struggling soul held fast in the grip of a deeply contradicted moment. And when it is done, being gently set down into the world like a fragile, winged creature caught for a moment in an exquisitely painful conundrum, before being released into the blue-gold of an endlessly shimmering arc of life.

Peripheral consciousness permits this kind of seeing through to the heart of things. It liberates the creative imagination from the grip of the rational mind so it can roam freely into the deeper inner spaces of being or into far-reaching, transcendent realms to grapple with angels and demons alike. Here, we need to open ourselves to the mystery of things and be willing to think magically. We need to invite our rational selves to stand down just for a while. In that quiet, sacred circle watched over by Grandmother Oak while the sun and storm gods convene in a gunmetal sky, I invite us all to become creatively imagining and magically thinking women.

I remind us all that this carefully prepared sacred space is a Spirit-charged realm inhabited by beings other than human who are intensely interested and vetted in the human experience, beings whose presences we become conscious of peripherally. It is where revelations and visions may be had directly or through inner dialogues with our helping spirits or allies of all kinds.

If we look closely with the eyes of the Self into any created thing, we see that it is permeated with tiny apertures revealing infinite things that cannot be named. Great and small divinities incarnate within this state of consciousness, corresponding to the need of the moment and engage the process at hand according to the Self's longings. The work of the Self toward individuation, toward her own spiritual completion, is multi-dimensional, occurring simultaneously in the parallel worlds of mind, body, and soul. It is peripheral consciousness that permits this simultaneity of transformative experience in multiple spheres of awareness. I encourage each Fire sister to dialogue freely with and about whatever Spirit-sourced entities, complexes, memories, or visions might come up for her during the ritual.

So, we begin to complete the preparation of the ritual setting. Remember that I have left sections and spaces in the arbor to be designed and set by each Fire sister according to her own vision. After adding ritual items at the base of Grandmother Oak, the Fire sisters set about creating their own personal altars around the arbor. They each choose a personal orientation, East, South, West, or North and place their ritual items around the individual altars I have created to honor each direction. They dedicate each directional altar with invocations and prayers as I sing a Directions Song.

❧❧❧❧

We move toward the Sacred Oak. She is to be dedicated and called forth by each Fire sister who names the oak according to her vision of what the tree is to signify for her this day. Grandmother Oak is how she made herself known to me earlier in the day. It will be the same for each Fire sister for we bring our own unique selves and purpose of soul to this ritual and none will impose her own on the other. Instead, we embrace and celebrate the distinctive gifts that we each bring to the Fire rite.

I begin the invocation as an illustration for the other sisters to follow. Trust, truth-telling, and permitting one's own inner inspiration to speak are keys to opening the doors to the world of Spirit and soul. I name and acknowledge my spiritual boon companions who have remained a steadying and guiding force throughout my life. It has been a journey fraught with a complex of anxieties described by ego-centered inflation on the one hand and inferiority on the other, self doubts on one end of the spectrum and irrefutable certainties on the far side. Epic weights of courage push me toward some shining something yet are underscored by an overwhelming fear as constant as a healthy heartbeat. My own soul torments are tempered both with divine raptures and revealed darker truths that have turned this life on Earth into a formidable penance. I share a vision at the Sacred Oak that I experienced earlier this morning before the Fire sisters arrived.

> *I am a Norsewoman transported to a place and time where I arrive from afar to offer greetings to the fraternal-twin deities Freya and her twin brother Freyr. I am at the sanctified center of the world for the ancient People of the North where Yggdrasill, the World Tree, stands. I offer a mixture of sweet red wine and honey and circle Yggdrasill with black stones.*

I talk about Yggdrasill as the supreme living metaphor for the ordered universe in all its multiplicity. Standing by Grandmother Oak, along with a thousand singing cicadas, I affirm the Norse shamans' knowledge of the inherently segmented nature of human being and of the necessary journey of the Self toward her wholeness, toward a noble ending. I sing an ode to a bygone age, a wisdom tradition that is yet mysteriously and fully present within my own Self. I speak of my abiding love of the great Icelandic epic sagas that tell of Viking heroes and heroines, of Norse gods and goddesses. I describe the sacred journey of life as the seeking soul strides across the great lengths of Yggdrasill, beginning in Hel where Fire burns in the great heart of Earth and on up through higher worlds to Asgardh, where the halls of Heaven shine resplendent.

And, I note the archetypal presence of the twinned and or trinitarian deities who have been constellated into my experience throughout this whole encounter with Fire and the ritual. I now include the powerful Norse trinity: Odin, Freyr and Freya in my sphere of ritual acknowledgments by Grandmother Oak. I talk about Odin being a manifold god who can assume any shape or role that becomes necessary to fulfill or maintain the created universe.

According to historian and runemaster, Edred Thorsson, Odin is called "the Alfadopl—Father, because he is the source of consciousness among the gods and mankind. His gift is the expanded human consciousness." In this sense, the individual is called not to worship an external god, but rather to develop enough of a sense of Self in relationship to and with the Divine that he or she can eventually come to embody god-consciousness, which is the longed-for gift, the goal of individuation. Like my beloved Minoan goddess who reveals herself as Artemis, Ishtar, or Eleyetheria, depending on the moment at hand, Freya too, is a three-fold goddess.

In the solitary depths where we deal with our own demons or divines, we may come to know the mythic language codes and inflated styles of communication that an archetype or a god or goddess understands and responds to. This day with Fire requires the company of a goddess who oversees magic. Some of the Fire sisters might need to do battle this day and warriors from the North look to Freya as their benefactress and protector. She is also a goddess of transformation. Thorssen tells us that "she can bring things into being, can cause them to become, and can cause them to pass away toward new beginnings." She is a Creatrix in her own right. Her companion and lover is her brother Freyr, "the Lord." Even more intimately, Freyr grew out of Freya's side and as such is also a constituent aspect of this most worthy goddess. Look, the rules just don't apply when you are a god or a goddess! Then, like the gentle Ganesha gazing on us from his altar in the West, beautiful Freya is also greatly concerned with peace, prosperity, abundance, and wellbeing for humans. Each Fire sister is precisely in need of each of these realities in her life. I ask in my invocation by the Sacred Oak that the combined qualities of all these great deities come into play for each of us according to our needs at this time.

I share with the Fire sisters that, when I came out of my vision early this morning, I looked at the Sacred Oak in the arbor and understood she was also to take the form of Yggdrasill for me. Her twin trunks rising straight and true toward the storm-filled sky would host the presences of my beloved Freya and Freyr. Again, we find a Trinity: the Sacred Oak, a god, and a goddess. I ask Yggdrasill, now embodied for me by the Sacred Oak, to keep us safe during the Fire ritual as we move between the worlds.

As I end my invocation with a runic invocation, splashing milk mixed with honey on Yggdrasill, the wind rises and rushes the arbor, raining leaves of gold. Nature is the sign language of the gods and of the One Supreme Divine. God speaks to us through Earth's own voice. Her Nature is the only sacred text whose *meaning* remains unadulterated by man no matter how much he degrades, pillages, and destroys her body.

With the final placement of small pieces of black obsidian encircling the base of the Sacred Oak, it is done. Each Fire sister then makes her own invocation, sharing from the heart her own personal greeting. We complete the Tree Dedication Rite by chanting a few simple vocables or sacred sounds that are carried to the heavens on a sweet melody.

Remember please, we are not worshipping trees here! We are giving praises and thanksgiving to the Creator and Divine Source of all existence who exists simultaneously within and beyond creation. We acknowledge all of creation's life forms as alive and intelligent, albeit in ways we shall never understand, but as such, Self-aware. We acknowledge that there are worlds and dimensions of existence that contain life forms, intelligences, and their own natural laws that are beyond the capacity of our reasoning minds to comprehend. And, we affirm that it is possible to communicate with these life forms and experience these dimensions with the faculties of the soul.

Now we turn away from the Sacred Oak and make our way to the fire pit in the center of the arbor. The Fire sisters have all been introduced to the ritual items and sacred food offerings on the tables. We first must dedicate the fire pit to make it ready to receive the Fire as natural element, and as the Divine embodied. All of these ritual activities are carried out with the grace of an inspired dance and with spontaneous words, whose affects inscribe themselves into our hearts and souls.

Each sister invites the spirit of Fire to approach and become present in the form in which it has appeared to her over the four weeks of preparation. This is an impassioned moment for us all because, for the first time, Fire is being personified, is named aloud, described, and introduced in a unique form as seen and experienced by each of us. Suddenly, the sun breaks out through the encircling stands of oaks, brightening a sky that refracts through leaves of gold into shards of turquoise. We speak, and the sky smiles.

Before we begin to build the Fire, each sister reverently places foods and other gifts in the fire pit as welcome offerings. In silence, we build a pyramid, beginning with kindling, cedar planks, and then oak logs to "house" the Fire. When it is ready, each sister lights the Fire simultaneously from each of the four directions. I sing a Spirit Calling Song that lingers in the air like thunder slowly rolling into the distance.

The flames surge, blue and purple, the colors of spirit and mystery, and we understand that Fire, in accepting our invitation, has become present in its most sovereign colors. In celebration, we pick up our ritual instruments, drums, rattles, and clapper sticks, and dance around the now roaring flames, singing a greathearted chant led quite rightly by Kit, who is working at finding her hidden voice and here bravely lets it be heard. It is difficult for her, but we patiently and lovingly follow her hesitant lead, respecting the painful effort showing itself in her trembling voice and the out of step drumbeat. We dance and sing with her and for her until she settles into the melody of the chant and into the rhythm that will guide her drum. Soon, the arbor is resounding with four voices attuned and in harmony, the wind chasing the flames into a whirl of red-gold with the Fire roaring its appreciation.

So, we begin our Fire rite as the magic of the moment takes hold like a fine, blue morning mist shot through with the red and gold of a fast approaching new day. The enchantment deepens and we become pilgrims circling meditatively around Fire at the sacred center of things. We move gracefully toward and around the Fire, toward and around our soul-Selves, and toward the Divine, like an arrow shot straight from the heart. We walk or dance in ritually set patterns around the arbor, circling the altars and Grandmother Oak.

As we rhythmically draw into and away from the Fire, as we begin to move more freely, more spontaneously, directed by an inner impulse or at the behest of a soul-inhabiting being, the ritual pathways established within the arbor begin to take on a propelling energy that is palpable, like walking into a bright spring wind. Now enchantment takes on a special hue, and the reparative healing begins. The arbor reflects a captivating, peripheral world experienced uniquely by each Fire sister in the midst of her own soul work.

At some moments, I am situated simultaneously at the edge of and inside the heart of the world. At others, I see my Self already present at the beginning of the end of time as I reach back to reclaim my archaic Self while dancing my future Self into a re-envisioned destiny. It is the spell of the Nataraj, the great cosmic dance of life. We surrender willingly to the transformative power and affects constellated into the microcosmic reflection of the universe that we have created in this very humble oak grove, in Indian Country, on sacred ground.

It is time now to delve into each of the Fire sisters' own experiences in preparing for, enacting, and then processing the Fire ritual. We will do this by resourcing the extraordinarily rich and provocative narratives they share with us in their poetry, and journal segments, in what I call the Fire texts. They are presented without any correcting of literary style so the original content that layers so poetically into the stream of consciousness wordplay that falls on the pages is retained and the mythopoesis involved may take full hold of you.

As I have done throughout this work so far, I will amplify each Fire sister's experience to deepen the discussion. One thing you will notice in most of the Fire texts is that the focus rests almost exclusively on the preparation phase leading up to the Fire ritual itself and, to some extent, its aftermath. In fact, it is common that the deepest of spiritual encounters often do not lend themselves well to everyday language. They are experiences of a kind that literally go beyond words. As one of my Fire sisters so eloquently puts it, "Our Fire Ceremony was so graceful and strong! [It] just seemed to come together so naturally, intuitively. I prefer not to speak directly of the ritual itself, because of respect for the mystery of it. But, as a whole it was <u>so beautiful</u>."

CHAPTER **FOUR**

The Poem

LUNA'S HAIR IS golden, her eyes are sea-deep blue, and she speaks with a lovely, lilting voice that reveals the Irish songstress. She is a devout, practicing Catholic while at the same time "walking the Red Road," the spiritual path indigenous Native America walks. Her experience leading up to and during the Fire ritual is profoundly alchemical. It leads to spiritual encounters in the midst of her own *nigredo:* her "dark night of the soul" that give birth to a poem of ultimate significance.

The poem becomes a catalyst, and the words enlivening it erupt through Luna's life like a shot of molten gold in a cave too deep to fathom or an articulated lifeline tossed to a gentle woman fallen into an irascible sea, or again, like a circle of strong helping hands reaching down to lift her from a fall too dire to recover from on her own. "For words," Hillman reminds us, "are persons." "Like angels," he says, words "are powers which have invisible power over us. They are personal presences which have whole mythologies: genders, genealogies, histories, and vogue; and their own guarding, blaspheming, creating, and annihilating effects." Luna's gestational journal writings leading up to the emergence of her poem are a testament to the breadth, the depth, and the intensity of her willingness to engage with the process that initiated within her Self and her life as a result of her promised intention to participate in the Fire ritual.

Entry 1:

> *Illness: I signed Ismana's consent form today. Thought I'd be keeping notes for a couple of weeks already, but most of that time, I've been sicker than I have ever been: ear infections, loss of hearing … the antibiotics are finally clearing a path. So much of the Fire in me has gone out, just extinguished by worry, fears, and exhaustion.*

Luna becomes very ill within days of agreeing to participate in the Fire ritual, and she remains so during the weeks leading up to it. We all walk wounded in this world or, to put it in Hillman's terms, the soul cannot exist without its afflictions.

Luna's wound, at least the one needing attention in the most immediate sense, is the fact of the Fire dying in her soul. She sees this reflected in the stagnation she is experiencing in her lived life. The lack of Fire in the heart, her lack of energy in stepping out into life, and a lack of spiritedness of soul eventually begin to express itself through her body, precisely in her left ear. She finds herself unable to hear, both physically and inwardly.

When one has made a formal commitment to an Earth-centered *rite de passage*, as this Fire ritual is for all of us, one has called out to the world of Spirit and Earth-in-her-Angel to draw close, to tend to us. The danger lies in our own lack of consciousness and intuitive knowing that when we send out such an invitation we should be crystal clear as to *who* is receiving that invitation. If we are not fully aware of our own actions or intentions, we have no idea *who* or *what* might be magnetized to our endeavor. We may find ourselves victims of our own best intentions to grow and evolve. We may experience our efforts being twisted and thwarted no matter how zealously we work toward our own individuation.

When we direct a heart-felt cry to the universe for guidance and protection as we strive for knowledge of Self and the workings of the Divine within we must be willing to surrender something of ourselves. But, it is in this *giving over* that the very real dangers lie if we are not fully certain as to what or to whom we are surrendering ourselves for repair, renovation, healing, and growth. It is not an easy task to tend to one's own spiritual need to grow into wholeness, certainty, and the joy of knowing union with the Divine. It takes courage and tenacity, stringent loyalty to Self, and the willingness to place our lives, even our sanity on the line: a warrior's unflinching stance.

My own Earth-centered philosophical position insists on the unified essence of all living beings. From this perspective, as mentioned earlier, I understand the human body as representing all of creation in microcosmic terms. As such, it symptomatically reflects the degrees of healthful connection or separation from Earth and the Divine as expressed in terms of sickness or health.

We may understand Luna's recurring ear infections and subsequent loss of hearing as the result of an invasion of bacterial or viral creatures out to conquer and colonize new and fertile territories. This would be true. We may also view Luna's suffering from the perspective of her Self who is laboring under a deep disconnect from Spirit and Earth precisely in her life-generating form as Fire.

You see the wound itself is a living thing. It has its own agenda, its own peculiar intelligence. It can become an activated psychological complex constellating to itself a community of archetypes or spirit beings attracted by nature to its particular gravitational field. In this case, the implosive draw of a Fire dying in the soul is the complex.

The wound may also bespeak deeper and older things. Depth psychologist Dennis Slattery describes his own living wound as a "trace of the memory, what I have left of the experience; it also marks the place of what I would call deep memory, an indelible recollection that one feels always at the edge of the field of consciousness."

For Luna, opening herself to the internal process of change instigated by her readiness to engage deeply with Fire necessitates resourcing memories that release on the one hand warm, loving, comforting images, and on the other hand, profoundly disturbing painful mindsets. However, if one is conscious and fully aware of one's intentions and their possible consequences, it is rare that an inner journey of this magnitude does not elicit boon companions in both spiritual and mundane terms. Again, we are never alone. Luna's brave intentions to embark on this journey to search for the tools necessary to reignite her subsiding inner Fire attract powerful female archetypes sourced from the world of symbol, metaphor, and Spirit: saints, goddesses, other spiritual beings, and Earth as Mother.

Entry 2:

A woman friend was here last night. It's been a year since we've seen each other. There's always been something re-markably inner worldly about our connection, and as we see each other so seldom, it only brightens that feeling and ex-perience. It's a sacramental time. Over dinner, she brought a Grace from the Carmelite Mystic, Teresa de Avila, and inward we went. She spoke of the interior journey of her own past year and of seeking the balance between writing a book and being consumed by it. I too, spoke of my own year and in the manner of looking deeply, as I spoke, I felt a kind of clarity and focus about the past year.

When we saw each other one year ago, I was at the begin-ning of what has turned out to be the most psychologically excruciating year of my life. I had been praying to shed my persona and it seems my prayers were answered in repeated, relentless bouts of a life under review, one episode after the next reaching all the way back to into my childhood, wher-ever I saw myself in the most failed and horrible identity. And, it just wouldn't let up. Ultimately my sense of my self worth was deeply eroded and that inner Fire, virtually extinguished. And yet, I've also felt, only in the experience of this physical illness, which has also been so debilitating not only fierce, but also an inner Peace and self-acceptance again. This demise of persona and autobiography started last May 02. It was May

9 this year that Ismana invited me to participate in this Fire ritual. It was May 19 that I became so physically ill.

There has always been something of the soulful adventuress about Luna. Her penchant for descending into frequent occurrences of deep, inner exploration usually results in a burst of literary creativity and a sense of accomplished Self-evolution.

Feminist scholar Carol Pearson assures us that "consciously taking one's journey, setting out to confront the unknown, marks the beginning of life lived at a new level." In the case of her inner preparation for the Fire ritual, Luna's journey is part and parcel of her conscious attitudinal stance toward the imperative of Self-development. It means doing the work of transforming from a lukewarm and disheartened individual, a relatively recent development, to reclaiming the woman she knows herself to be. Like St. Theresa of Avila a woman of certain courage, aflame with a passion for life and for God, generative and joyful.

St. Teresa of Avila, a 16th century Spanish Carmelite mystic celebrated for the fierceness of her convictions and her ardent love of Christ and his Mother, emerges into Luna's life in this moment via a discussion with a good friend. Remember the very real power and meta-functionality of words. This is a grace of the highest order. Both Luna and I share an abiding love of St. Teresa, who is now fully present in our respective spheres of consciousness and intent. She as experiencer and recorder, and I as reader and responder. This is how we become caught up in and constellated to each other's complexes!

St. Teresa arrives, as do all benevolent spirits and saints who are worth their metal, bringing a gift of grace. It is a gift that Luna yearns for: a God-sourced Fire in the soul.

The word fierce is derived from the Old French word *fer*, or *fier* meaning strong, wild, brave, proud, and mighty. Reflecting St. Teresa's ardent devotion for Christ as Savior and Lord, Luna must take herself to places in the heart where the warm ardor of love rises unbounded like the sun wrapping a translucent veil of golden light around his beloved dawning Earth. She needs to live ardently, love fiercely, and pursue her own evasive Fire like a lover who will simply not brook the loss of her beloved. The Old French word *ardure,* from which the word ardor is derived, tells of the heat of desire and the glow of the flame, the Fire of courage, eagerness, and the zeal to move mountains for the sake of a dream.

What is a grace in the sense that we are using it for Luna? It is a spiritual gift. It refers to a God-inspired state of being. So it is that St. Teresa comes to us through Luna with her own way of understanding the journey toward an illuminated and Self-aware soul. Insisting on the importance of Self-knowledge as a means for learning to exist in God's grace, and at the same time knowing how difficult a task it is for the human soul to deal with Self-knowledge, St. Teresa says, "Even if you were raised right up to the heavens, you should never relax your cultivation of it."

Key to the process of attaining to this state of grace is the cultivation of a love grounded in surrender. St. Teresa uses the words Self-knowledge and humility equivalently, because for her, the path to Self-knowledge in the grace of God *is* the path of humility. In doing the work of the soul, we must practice humility. St. Teresa's message to Luna and to the Fire sisters is this, "Strive always to move forward on the spiritual path … it simply is not possible that a soul who has come this far would stop growing. Love is never idle."

As her journal testifies, Luna is constantly reminded of the magic and mystery involved in tending to the soul. Jung would describe her as having precisely the alchemical attitude necessary to achieve authentic individuation: a readiness to undergo permanent transformation. She is willing to surrender herself to the painful process of inner disintegration and re-integration required for the inner conversion of a fast-fading Fire in the soul to the full-bodied flame she is longing for.

Almost immediately after making her formal intention to participate in the Fire ritual, she begins to experience a severe psychophysical dismantling of a lukewarm persona that is no longer of service to her Self. In the heart of her dying Fire complex, in the midst of inner and outer chaos, Luna finds herself in a frightening void where the known seems irretrievably lost and the unknown too close for comfort.

True change within a person's inner and outer life often requires an intimate turbulent interaction between emotional chaos and quiet order. Ideally, this interaction should occur in a safe place, a ritual setting, in the company of allies and boon companions, whether it be one's therapist, support group, spiritual circle, or spirit community. Remember that it is the journey toward enlightenment and wholeness of being that provides a constant guideline for a life lived with depth and purpose. As Luna begins the process of ritualizing her preparation for the Fire ritual, her personal dedications reflect both the depth of her engagement and the immediacy of the response from the realm of Spirit, from Earth Mother, and from her own soul.

Entry 3:

Mid-life, rebirth: Could it be that this ritual might serve to rekindle that Fire again? As a mid-life woman perhaps offering her past to the flames but not her future?

Dedication: I would long to somehow rededicate myself to helping that inner Fire to get going again.

Initiation: Celtic goddess: It occurred to me this morning that Brigid, the Celtic goddess of poetry, of Fire, of the hearth, is somehow an initiation for me into the first notes of this Fire -ritual journal. It hadn't occurred to me about Brigid, Keeper of the Eternal Flame—Poet until today.

Naming: To rekindle it (the inner Fire) with my Sisters from the Four Directions. Not only for myself, no, never that. It's without that inner Fire that I feel most alone, selfish. "Kin" is the root of "kindle."

And the South, I also have such a sense of poetry being connected through the South.

I feel I've just heard chimes in my clogged left ear. How could that be? My little chimes hang in the window, facing South. Maybe an echo of the South's response to my longing?

Luna's "feeling" that she hears chimes in her deaf ear echoing from the South, her poetic sense of connection with that cardinal direction and with Brigid, the ancient Irish goddess of sacred poetry, Fire and the hearth underscores an important reality. The dramatic forms that Spirit takes as it stories itself up from the depths of the human soul out into the bright light of day via our creative imagination. Again, I do not use the term creative imagination in its mundane sense referring to inconsequential fancies or romantic fantasies but in the alchemical sense, the *imaginatio vera:* a true faculty of the soul used to personify what are fundamentally divinely inspired revelations or insights, and thus form meaningful relationships with them. St. Theresa, Brigid, the South, Fire, chimes. These images, symbolic or metaphorical, provide "bodies" for certain entities to reside in for the time and purpose allotted to them in a given situation. It then becomes important for the individuating soul to discover not only his or her intimate associations with these invisible spiritual forces or complex archetypal patterns but also their relationship to and with each other. We see this happening for Luna as she engages with her own Fire dying in the soul complex.

Peripheral consciousness, as discussed early on, entails the continual inner and outer acknowledgement of these intimate associations. Profound insights, enlightenments, grace-filled moments, flashes of joy in the midst of inexplicable sadness, visions and mysteries, banked sufferings suddenly surfacing, all these constitute one's intimate associations with the soul and the Divine revealed. On so many levels, Luna's synergy with all that comprises her conscious experience of searching for her lost flame is a wonderful example of the connective bridging function of peripheral consciousness.

When a despairing and solitary soul cries out to the universe for authentic change, for new life and light, a sympathetic resonance *always* signals its response. This begs the question: are we listening and will we be able to recognize let alone reach for the helping hand? For the most part no, since making that move means undertaking the extremely difficult task of resolving, changing, and permanently letting go of whatever is no longer of use or significance in our lives, then to move forward.

For those who do undertake this daunting prospect the sympathetic resonance responding to our call builds to varying degrees of intensity and complexity. And it is precisely in this resonation that we identify who or what has heeded our call. This is key. When we acknowledge these resonating presences, welcoming them by name, celebrating their own life stories and teachings, they are able to serve as guides on our journey or healers of the particular wound that needs tending.

For Luna, this sympathetic resonance images itself in multiple personifications during her preparation for and participation in the Fire ritual. Influential psychodynamic spiritual symbols, signs, and spirit beings gather in support of her process as she seeks to discover the "kindling" with which she can enliven the dying flame flickering precariously within her own soul. Their essential purpose is to unite the oppositional dynamics that regularly unbalance all of us in our lives as described so eloquently in Luna's experience.

Entry 4:

I drove to St. D's for the Sunday evening Mass. Celebrating today: the Ascension. Anyway, on the way in, I stopped and sat in front of a statue of Our Lady in her white robes with blue sash and her crown of golden stars. There she was, standing with her outstretched arms, in a quiet, private grotto. I was facing the South as I sat there quietly in front of her. A tall votive candle was placed at her feet, its flame flickering strongly, dancing in the breeze. This encounter just after my question,

"How do I welcome you back, Sacred Fire? I turn to the South
to ask you this question."

I don't yet fully understand the response, but I know the
above speaks to my heart regarding the question, the Fire,
the direction. Thank you. May I honor the mystery and not
so much to unravel but to behold— "Magnificat Anima Mea."

4 Spirit Women: Also, life continues to beckon. I realize the
4 Spirit Women who call my heart so strongly: Brigid and Our
Lady, as I've mentioned, and also Mary Magdalene, and White
Buffalo Calf Woman—a tall votive for each—the kindling of
Sacred Fire to illumine each of their mysteries? Poetry. Peace,
love and keeping sacred. These qualities are just flickers of
seeing into their presence. The Fire of the Illuminating Word,
The vigil Fire of the Queen of Peace, The Fire of Magdalene's
impassioned love for Jesus and His for her, the Fire of Prayer—
carried, lit, offered in Sacred Ceremony for the People.

Keeping this Fire going, feeling its strength in the simple
flame of a poem, a votive, a heart in love, a lighter to a Sacred
Pipe lifted in Prayer. These small, kept flames are powerful
enough to rekindle the heart. But I feel they must be kept with
devotion. I sense the intuitive movement toward the personal
Fire ritual that Ismana asked us each to bring, and my sense of
bringing in these Sacred Women from the South to the ritual.
Yes. This is the Direction I go to, to pray for women, for all
souls, and for guidance through dream, song, silence, craft,
poetry, and prayer.

Thank you, dear Sacred Women, for coming into relationship for me in this way. May I know you and what you reveal,
what you veil. I hope that a poem might come. We shall see.
I'm beginning to glimpse some things to do.

Luna's articulation of her experience as she begins to negotiate
her dying Fire complex underscores the dynamic nature of the archetypal patterns and presences called to the service of her individuating

soul. She responds accordingly by embracing the signs of their intentional presence and, we might say, "personal" interest in her process of tending to her own soul's needs. In fact, Luna 's ease with articulating her inner and outer experience in symbolic, archetypal, and poetic terms emphasizes a way of being-in-the-world that magnetizes archetypal involvement and interaction with the Divine. It is a mythical consciousness by which we name, clothe, and give personality and purpose to an image or felt presence so we may establish the right relationship with it. This relationship, like a bolt of lightning, may ignite our own process of Self-transformation. Again, these images may arise from within, representing an aspect of our own multidimensional Self, or they may be beings who exist in worlds other than our own, and who function independently yet in relation to us from *their* side of things.

Personification is an essential feature of soul work in both its shadowed and illuminated operations. Luna's Shadow is certainly playing a significant part in the process at hand. Be warned. The Shadow is, more often than not, the smart one with a good mind and a tendency toward genius. Love your own Shadow into the sunlight. Cultivate her loyalty to your own soul's dream of the Light and she will give up her own life for yours in the darkest hour. This is also a grace.

Luna's beautifully faceted experience illustrates this personifying process in vivid terms. We are introduced to Brigid, the Celtic goddess of poetry, also the goddess of Fire whose directional orientation is the South. Then there is the beloved of the Nazarene, Mary Magdalene—otherwise forbidden fruit. Mary, the Virgin Mother of the Divine Child, has appeared, as has White Buffalo Calf Pipe Woman of the Great Plains, an ancient spirit being who brought the Seven Sacred Rites to the Lakota nation. And, Marilyn Monroe, a celluloid Fire goddess in her own right! In fact, they are all Luna in terms of representing to her those aspects of her own being that resonate perfectly with their own. However, as independent entities they are also here on their own terms and for their own reasons.

Entry 5:

A Fire goddess! She's flashing a smile that melted all hearts, golden hair, hot and sexy, sweetly vulnerable, and all too fragile. It's Marilyn Monroe's birthday. A woman upon whom infinite projections were cast, like so many evil spells that seemingly destroyed her in the process.

Invocation: May your spirit be free, infinitely beautiful, and always true.

Illness: I keep waiting for this illness to abate so that I can more fully give myself, but after an uneasy "flare-up" in the ears, it seems I need to fully come into this ritual and journal as an ill person in deep need of healing. I've begun to feel a little bit scared and at a time when I feel least "in control" and very vulnerable.

The treatments so far have seemed to do very little with healing. The illness itself may have healing in it, but I've yet to realize how, other than that my depletion on so many levels may have finally called me to the table.

Invocation while lighting sage: "Fire, Fire where are you? Am I too wet for you? Drowning? It may be so. How do I welcome you once more within me with your soft, vibrant blue-gold light in the heart, in the thought, in the body? The South, the dream direction, women's direction, Spirit Road direction, I turn to you—toward you. I've so long been gifted with dream guidance, yet during this illness, next to nothing. How do I welcome you back Sacred Fire? I turn to the South to ask you this question. May I listen deeply, deeply to your response ... I can hardly hear anything on the outside now. Perhaps I might still be able to listen within.

Falling into a depression can often be a productive move on the part of the seeking soul and Luna is willing to go there. Marie Louise von Franz tell us that an individual experiencing this kind of constructive depression often feels as if he or she is being "pressed down, compressed, usually because a part of the psychological libido is below and has to be fetched up; the real energy of life has fallen into a deeper layer of the personality and can only be reached through a depression."

"Go deeper and deeper," she encourages us, "until you again reach the level of psychological energy where some creative idea can come out and suddenly, at the bottom, an impulse of life and creativeness which has been overlooked may appear."

This is good. In order to keep from being distracted by her physical illness, Luna reorients toward the South direction. It is there that she focuses her prayer for recollection, renewal, and rebirth within the matrix of the flickering flame in her soul desperately in need of re-ignition, desperately in need of a new direction.

The South has now taken on a three-fold form: a trinitarian archetype representing the dream, the spirit path, and women's ways. It points to a renewed world of hope, possibility, creativity, and the actualization of Luna's search for kindling to feed the dying flame. The South has also become a ritually designated orientation, a containing space in which she may safely tend to the wounds around which her Fire dying in the soul complex has built a fortress to defend itself. The South becomes the focal point in the heart of her burning need to become inflamed, to reclaim the fiery legacy by which she once referenced herself. But Luna must first come to grips with her fears.

Entry 6:

 Fear of Fire & the South—hell—dangerous: I was raised to fear Fire, and when I think about it, the "South" as well. Brought up to consider Fire dangerous in an earthly sense ("don't let children play with matches!"), but especially in the eternal sense: Fire meant Hell. In childhood fairytales, dragons breathed Fire. I think it's mostly in that inner, eternal sense that my fear of Fire really took hold. I can think of so many benign encounters with Fire growing up that didn't shake that fear for a second: birthday candles, campfires, sparkles, fire flies.

Entry 7:

Summer Solstice. This has always been my favorite season; something always rises up in me, mostly in the sense of irrepressible body memory. It is a joyful body memory, particularly all the teenage years and all those long, sweet summers outdoors. Woods, lakes, horses, stars. And so many stars above those beautiful Southern Indiana hills! And every summer that joy rises up. But now, the extinguishing in me has translated as a sadness in recent years. When the summer comes and I feel that rising then there is a plummet, a deflation. Perhaps this is the summer to restore that connection again via this longed for rekindling. I was born in the summer. I do connect Fire and summer in a strong way. There is a sense of Fire in winter too, but summer has the heart of it for me. Summer campfires over the years took on a ritual meaning. Every night, circling around the Fire, all eyes on the crackling flames and, inevitably, all eyes looking inward too as the Fire calls us to do.

I did not fear Fire then. I loved her, and I felt her take me inward, and I felt her draw us into a vibrant circle around her. That's where it began. But after years of being taught to fear the Fire of God's wrath in the darkness of Hell, I can see even now the peril to one's Spirit of living in fear, in dread. The fear of the inner Fire, the Shadow of that, extinguishes one. I'm not articulating this quite right and I need to because I'm onto something important I think for this rekindling of being to happen. Somehow, the learning of so many fears was left behind when I went to camp—learned something <u>else</u> there, recognized something else and my spirit came so alive—connected w/Fire, Earth, Water, Air, one's self! How remarkable that 3 of

*the Fire Women within that I feel so drawn to are "from" the
traditions that taught me fear! Fear of the Fire included. Yet,
these Sacred Spirit Women are with me and besides the possibility of rekindling, there is also, I feel, the possibility of reconciling with my fears rather than running from them or being
consumed by them. Who knew this Fire quest would illumine
such questions or such autobiography?*

Entry 8:

*And "the South"—a subtler fear but also earthly and un-
earthly childhood lessons learned. "The South" was a place
where there was segregation, prejudice and worse. Not that
these things didn't also exist in Indiana! But I want to, need to
acknowledge this genealogy of meaning.*

Entry 9:

*This journal itself is the South direction too: the inner di-
rection, the intuitive direction. It is a map for traveling to the
South. It is also a guide to going inside, to reveal a living on the
outside that loves to keep step w/mystery. How wonderful to
sense that alignment! How dulling when I don't. I remember
finding my way in the dark at camp. Finding my way now feels
like my life depends on it. Seeking that inner Fire light—so, so
beautiful in the darkness.*

Luna's South direction now begins to serve as a lens of perception through which she begins to comprehend the multilayered reality of her present circumstances. It also serves as a beckoning portal,
a threshold, through which she will finally envision her own healing
rites in the times leading up to and during the Fire ritual. In this sense
too, the South becomes for Luna "a guide to going inside to reveal a
living on the outside that loves to keep step w/mystery. How wonderful to sense that alignment!" she exclaims.

In both the Norse and Celtic cultures to which St. Brigid belongs,

Muspellsheimr, the Fire -World, lies in the South. It is here that the eternal Sacred Fire is produced whose sparks light up the starry heavens and where the Fire of creation blazes like a comet across a bewildered sky. It is also from *Muspellsheimr* that the gods throw lightning bolts across storm-strewn skies, thundering their divine displeasures. Our responsibility is to listen, tend to the issue, and move on.

Luna must also overcome another kind of cultural conditioning if she is to succeed in reaching for and lighting her own inner Fire , and she is well aware of what this means. "After years of being taught to fear the Fire of God's wrath in the darkness of Hell," she says, "I can see even now the peril to one's soul of living in fear, in dread. The fear of the inner Fire, the Shadow of that, extinguishes one."

This is key to the profound sadness permeating Luna's present tense. She must tend to the Marilyn Munroe residing within herself. If Marilyn, irresistible blonde bombshell with an angel's smile, represents the shadowed side of Luna's deeply diminished inner flame, then she must retrieve that shadowed aspect of herself, re-envision herself into a new kind of flaming beauty, and love that part of herself into being once more. She needs to rediscover herself *as* Fire goddess.

"She's flashing a smile that melted all hearts, golden hair, hot and sexy, sweetly vulnerable, and all too fragile," Luna says of Marilyn, who took the whole world by storm. And, understanding the price, Luna continues, "A woman upon whom infinite projections were cast, like so many evil spells that seemingly destroyed her in the process." Then, "<u>An Invocation to Marilyn:</u> May your spirit always be free; your beauty infinite, and always true." Is Luna's heartfelt invocation for them both?

Entry 10:
  A poem has started to come! Yesterday was Father's Day.
  It is a first draft, rough, but whole. I will offer the drafts, when
  the time comes, to the Fire in ceremony.

Entry 11:

> *The poem awaits more writing; but it's alive. It's my Solstice Fire Ceremony poem.*

Again, with the poetess Brigid as her muse and guide, the strongest vehicle for Luna's healing and Self-transformation becomes her poem. She conceives of it from the start as both a prophetic beginning to the whole process and its culmination. This is the alchemical process at its most powerful as described by the ancient symbol of the *uroboros,* often depicted as a serpent or dragon curved around in a full circle in order to consume its own tail, in other words, its own Self. "In childhood fairytales, dragons breathed Fire," a fearful Luna tells us. But, here and now, she must learn to overcome her learned fear of Fire. Instead, she needs to reach for the wisdom tradition that dragon as archetype holds and embrace its higher teachings on Fire. She must learn how to consume dragon Fire one breath at a time in the same way as one who survives in the barren desert wastes must take only small sips when the sweet nectar of life finally comes.

The dragon, as symbolized in the *uroborus,* may represent the beginning of an end or the end of a beginning. In the work of the soul, beginnings and endings nourish each other simultaneously. Each one of us feeds on "foodstuffs" produced by our own Self who in turn feeds on our ego-driven personality, which provides nourishment for the soul again in a food chain of the spirit. Our "soul food" is contained in the experiences of life itself. There is no more potent nutrient or toxin for the human being. It is how we become whom we are for better or worse.

Thus we cultivate our Selves, grow, blossom, mature, and then fade away in a never-ending cycle of life. Our physical beings have their beginning in our own star, the sun, itself the origin of Fire, of light, and of life on Earth. This is the meaning of the dragon consuming itself in a circle of life and death. This is also Luna's poem and all that it stands for.

Entry 12:

Trying to work on the poem—getting nowhere. The "real" poem underneath has yet to emerge. Frustrating! Sacred Fire, intuitive South, you will not be toyed with, constructed. May I not give up!

Entry 13:

Fire works! Ah Fire journal! It's been too long away from you. Work and hoping for a deeper, freer rendering of the poem draft have kept me quiet, contemplative. Little boons that now and then startle me. This journal is really taking me essentially through to the sacredness of the inner Fire. I'm having a sense growing about "my own" Ceremony within this Circle of Women. And I'm wondering if I may ask my Fire sisters when we gather on July 27, the 4 of us, to bring all our journeys together by each holding a votive for each of the 4 Inner Spirit Fire Women I have connected with on this journey of longed-for rekindling.

The sense of the South direction has become subtle. I feel like my intuitive access to Mary the Mother, Mary Magdalene, Brigid, and White Buffalo Calf Woman is particularly kind to this direction. And so, for my own 4th of July celebration, I hope to be able to discover the poem within, the poem that has yet to fully reveal herself. May she do so! May she do so!

The poem is just not happening. I don't like it. It is very hard. I may have to let it go. That makes me sad. It is the Sacred Craft I feel most alive in and I know when it's flowing. It's not. It's like the pilot light is out in me. Yes, maybe I have to let it go and maybe I can't give it up either! Will I have to hold the contradiction? Carry the kindling, carefully, watchfully, and mindfully. Maybe I'm putting my own ideas on "it," the process that is, too much and not allowing the poem to emerge on its own. The sense in me to feel a completion for this journal, this Fire Ceremony seems to really hinge on a *poem coming. A poem I feel alive in crafting, in being with, in being crafted by. In being the kindling and the Fire Keeper both. I must accept that it may not come. I hope with all my heart that it will.*

Entry 14:

I have not found my inner Fire. In fact, a week of worries and anxieties stoking up about this and other things has only dimmed the inner light. No poem as yet. And yet later, a little writing comes through, but this time as a supplicant.

Entry 15:

Another illness! The roof of my mouth is on Fire! Is the kindling of (my) poem stuck there, burning? To be sick again already is discouraging and very disturbing. Oh Fire Women within, oh sacred South, how do I respond? The little poem is much sweeter and whatever is ready or not by our collective Fire Ceremony coming up very soon, I will offer.

Entry 16:

Finally—the poem! Last night and I realize this morning it came through on the late evening of Mary Magdalene's Feast Day (today). I'm very grateful, moved deeply by the timing. So many drafts—this one emerged from them, underneath them all and quite different from the prior efforts, forms. Primarily it is the voice of the Mother quieting my own, gently. And she does ask for one Word and for much Listening.

The other matter is that I am ill again and the cause of it evading diagnosis and treatment. I hope, I pray that I'm well enough to join my sisters on Sunday for the Fire Ceremony. These times are so precarious, fraught. I'm discouraged. But the poem is medicine, is Medicine. I receive it with gratitude and I offer it with love. "Magdalena, whose Beloved freed her, healed her of all her demons, of a tortured mind, healed her wounded heart, healed her body of all trespassing, freed her spirit to genuine fidelity—may her Sacred Water be very near and honored."

In full cognizance Luna willingly suffers her own poem's conception, gestation, and the literary labor pains that mirror her own inner state. She is morbid, pallid, damp, and spiritless, and her lack of hearing compounds her situation. Her illness entrenches. She becomes more deeply depressed and struggles with a growing sense of depletion and desolation at the very core. But instead of trying to escape the disconnection, the feelings of alienation, loneliness, the growing chill in her own soul, she chooses to care for her soul. St. Teresa, St. Brigid, White Buffalo Calf Pipe Woman, the Magdalene, and the Virgin herself would simply not permit any other move. All are warriors and breakers of bondage respective to their own cultural realities and all stand fearless in the face of God precisely because they know how to fall to their knees in abject humility at just the right moment.

Depth psychologist Thomas Moore applauds this kind of positive turn, describing depression as a soul activity critical to the process of individuation. "Maybe we have to broaden our vision," he says, "and see that feelings of emptiness, the loss of familiar understandings and structures in life, and the vanishing of enthusiasm, even though they seem negative, are elements that can be appropriated and used to give life fresh imagination." Luna understands this and knows that the creative process of grappling with and writing the poem will reveal answers, insights, and the rehabilitation she needs to move beyond her present circumstances. The poem will propel her return to a life fired with an energetic sense of destined purpose, confidence, and direction. The poem itself is also the means through which the Four Sacred Women, in particular the Virgin, speak.

Entry 17:

Tonight is the 4th night since my 50th birthday. For the 4th night, I will sleep under the Sacred Turtle blanket. I also placed a new ring on my finger 4 days ago on my birthday. I have not worn a ring in many years. I intended to do these things on my birthday this year in a personal, private ceremony of re-birthing. As it happens, these 4 nights coincide between my birthday and our Fire Ceremony tomorrow. I feel so amazed and grateful by the timing of all this. I feel I have been given the opportunity to engage in a genuinely healing journey. No matter what may yet come, this will always be with me.

Fire Ceremony Offerings: I will offer all my drafts to the Fire.
I will pass the heart votive to each of my sisters to hold.
I will offer my poem aloud to each of my sisters with a flower candle.
And I will listen.

Luna arrives at the arbor this morning pale, somewhat fragile, yet also excited and with a celebratory air about her that is infectious. She is anxious to get started. She cannot wait to share her poem. In its conception, gestation, birth, and ultimate gifting to Fire and to the Fire sisters, the poem represents for her the culmination of a *rite de passage* of extraordinary significance.

In mythopoetic space, Marie Louise von Franz tells us, "one should see the part played by one's own complex ... all has to be taken back ... like a kind of death." We might say that the poem as an activated archetype serves as a hermetically sealed vessel inside which Luna is forced into a creative introversion. She must willingly undergo a transformation of temperament, attitude, and feeling leading to a kind of inner death symbolized by the dying Fire within, and then a rebirth with her poem as the kindling and her own promise to her Self serving as the igniting flame.

Luna and her poem are one being in the same way that an infant *in utero* is one with her mother. Her poem forms the alchemical chamber in which she is called to look deeply into herself from the outside in and from the inside out. From the moment of conception, knowing that a poem would be the key, she waits, fretting, wringing her hands, crying out for help, and sinking into a bittersweet alchemy of sorrow. Then there are jubilant thanks for small mercies when they do come, as her hesitant, poetic words tumble in blue ink onto yellow paper—the color of the sun making love to the sky in blue and gold. Ignition.

Luna commences her own unique ritual process. The Fire sisters stand close to the roaring Fire as we witness her mandalic circumambulation around the flames beginning at the South. Here Luna calls in the spirit-women who have accompanied her on this journey from the beginning and introduces them to us by name. She shares the meaning of the sacred circle for her, explaining what each directional altar signifies and why she has placed the personal objects she has brought with her at a particular direction in the arbor. She invokes images, spirits, and significances symbolized by each orientation of the ritual setting according to her own wisdom traditions. After acknowledging each directional altar, Luna gathers up food and herb offerings from the table set up as a ritual space for the purpose of "feeding" the Fire, offering them reverently to the flames.

Then sitting down on the ground close to the flames, she sets several sheets of yellow paper on the ground along with a small, white marble sculpture of the Virgin and Child encircled with four heart-shaped votive candles. She has brought to the flames her need to rekindle what she is experiencing as a dying Fire in her own soul. She asks for reconciliation and resolution of past sorrows and to move beyond a stagnating and confining life pattern.

The Fire sisters' hearts go out to her as we listen to her own heart's plea for rebirth and for the healing promise in new beginnings. We are seated in a semi-circle around what is actually a bonfire blazing waist high at some moments. Tongues of flame thrust out toward us, and I am reminded of dragon's breath. Blue smoke winding upward toward the heavens is shot with the silver rays of a sun struggling to break through a storm-filled sky.

As Fire Keeper, I constantly feed the flames with wood and ritual "foods" during Luna's activities. I am hoping for a gentle increase. But Fire has a mind of its own. It begins to blaze and crackle, giving birth to its own internal windstorm that soars, spinning the flames into a breathtaking spiral of ice blue, purple at the tip, while its heart burns red-gold turning snow white at its ashen core. I smile in quiet surrender.

As she begins to share her experience of preparing for the Fire ritual with us, Luna gathers into her hands the single sheets of yellow paper that bear the calligraphic mark of her poem in various stages of development. Curled up like a tender blossom at the feet of the Fire, with quiet dignity, she solemnly feeds each page to the blaze. These pages are Luna's formal gifts offered ritually to the Fire as a nutritive testament to the suffering she has endured while experiencing the gradual loss of her own inner flame over time. As the flames accept her calligraphic testimonial, flaring and curling around each yellow page they consume, she confirms aloud to all beings attending to us in the arbor, and to her Fire sisters, her willingness to undergo what-ever is necessary for a Spirit-guided change in her life. She asks for nothing less than a complete transformation at the deepest levels of being. We fall silent, gazing into the dancing flames.

When the sheets of yellow paper have been rendered into ash, as each hesitant phrase, each insecure word, each hurriedly scribbled alphabet becomes transmuted into living presences in the heart of the Fire, Luna hands out segments of the final version of her poem to each Fire sister to read aloud. Each of us is brought to tears as we read our stanza aloud, for the poem speaks universally to what is in all our hearts at this moment, in this sacred space, around a great-spirited Fire burning as brightly as the sun itself. Then Luna reads the whole poem aloud by herself.

We wait. The air becomes heavy and still.

She weeps her life. Her tears spill onto the pages, as she wrings her pale, slim hands. She sings and her voice trembles. Tears spring from our eyes for and with our Fire sister. Then the weeping ends. And the world watches.

We move into another long silence and move closer to the Fire, absorbing all sounds, scents, and sights. There are ongoing discussions among the birds and the butterflies. The wind and the trees are intimates and have much to say. Fire and all that it contains invites a greater concentration, a deeper reverie. There are insights and intuitions, revelations and guidance. Then it is done. Luna instructs each sister to feed her stanza to Fire, waiting until the page has been completely consumed before inviting the next sister to offer hers. We all observe the Fire 's particular and unique reaction to each page as it surrenders itself to the ever-eager flames.

Transcendentally, the poem speaks what is in each of the Fire sisters' hearts, addressing our deepest needs as we circle around the Fire during Luna's ritual. It houses goddesses and saints; a Virgin, and a beloved Whore, the Magdalene, made sacred by Divine love. It holds Earth in her Southern orientation and the Originator of the sacred rites of the indigenous Lakota peoples, White Buffalo Calf Pipe Woman. As ancient spirit and as Great Mother, it speaks of the dreaming soul and sacred promises.

The poem is a mythology. It has taken on *being*. We introduce ourselves to it. We understand its presence and respond to its own special life force. It turns and turns again gazing at each one of us with a question. It forces our attentiveness the way the Buddha means it to be: a soul-referenced Self on the alert. It causes the heart to wrench and tears to flow. It brings us to our knees. Not because it is a brilliant poem necessarily, and not necessarily because it transports us to transcendent realms or states of heightened consciousness, but because it is heartbreakingly simple and true to the nature of the soul of the poetess. It *speaks* to us from *its* own heart and touches each of us in a palpably mysterious way.

We are in awe since part of the preparation for this Fire ritual was making a commitment that none of us would communicate with each other prior to the day itself. None of us could know what each would bring, or how each would approach the Fire ritually. Nevertheless, Luna's poem encompasses and reflects all that each Fire sister brings for healing, to give voice to, in celebration of, to let go of, and to be released from.

Words as archetypes or persons form the very underpinnings of our conscious existence as they shape our own lives, personalities, and destinies. Depending on the nature of our invitation, they may appear as messengers, guardians and guides, boon companions or tricksters, teachers or distracters as we move toward either evolving into the best of ourselves or devolving into the worst.

The particular archetypes animating and residing in each word or word cluster in Luna's poem serve as independent carriers of soul between the Fire sisters. Words filled with Spirit and emotion spring off the pages toward each of us, urging us to embrace them as intimately and fully as does the poetess herself. They fill us, move us, direct us, nourish us, and we reciprocate in feeling and gestural response. Each word and poetic turn of phrase crystallizes Luna's experience—Jung says that crystals are the thoughts of God.

Participating in the Fire ritual is a completion of an extraordinary process for Luna. Using her poem as a transforming vehicle for change, inspiration, and rekindling, she successfully journeys out of her own personal malaise described by loss, grief, confusion, and marked by a fear that manifests in severe illness. Now freshly minted, she emerges with a rediscovered creativity into the radiance of a newly energized day. She has also become a beloved member of a new community of women with a passion for Fire. We may meet again or not, but the bond is secure and Fire has sealed the promise. The poem follows, and speaks for itself.

Devotional

Burning! The roof of her mouth
Where poems lodge and go up in smoke,
Extinguished
Before they ever reach the page.

Consumed life
In her nearing 50 years,
Looks both ways and
Wants to disappear like the last
Ember into ash.

Darkening, she sees
The sweet flame dancing
At the pure, stone feet of the Mother:

Give all your words into my care!
Let me turn them into silent prayer for you.
Cease to be a poet, a midlife woman.
Cease to be a regretter of being!

Become a listener, a devotional listener.
See the petals of Fire around my heart—
Of Love that will clean and rekindle you.

Fire women:
Marys, the 2 Marys—Mother
And Magdalene of Jesus,
And Brigid, whose pen en-chanted prayer.

And White Buffalo Calf Woman,
Whose Gift brings Light to the people
We will rekindle you.

You and Others whose light is dimming.

Our laughter and our tears
Will sparkle in the darkness for you
Like lanterns, like candles, like campfires,
Like votive flames quietly dancing with the dark.
We Fire women, we will rekindle you.
Look beyond the burning roof into the starlit night.

And Luna, you do not need to say anything
More than your own name
To find your way to the light in the dark.

The Flame

KIT COMES TO the Fire ritual, as do we all, believing that this event is the precise answer to a personal prayer. In spite of working full time at a high-pressure job and studying for her master's degree in transpersonal psychology, she is willing to commit herself to the soul work involved as she prepares for and then brings herself to the Fire ritual at Indian Canyon. She participates courageously in those aspects of the rites that challenge her most vulnerable fragilities.

During the ritual, Kit remains steady as a rock in a wildfire as Fire sister Spring rages in her Kali Ma, as Luna graciously and with quiet conviction shares her process and her poem, and as I break my heart, offering pieces to the Fire in exchange for an ultimately unattainable sense of belonging to a people by blood or geography. Kit shares what she has experienced over the past four weeks leading up to the Fire ritual, working from email correspondences that she has brought with her. Once again, we are in awe at the deepening levels of shared experience and the connectivity across space and time between us all. Abandonment, loneliness and alienation, and a desperate longing for authentic, loving relationships rise to the surface for each of us.

It bears repeating that the soul's perspectives on the vicissitudes of the life lived are often revealed through dreams and visions and spoken in the language of Nature and Spirit as signs, symbols, and synchronicities. It is a language critical for us to learn or relearn and to which we must pay close attention. For many, it requires the redis-covery and development of the faculties of intuition and instinct in relation to and with Nature and Spirit.

Earth-in-her-Angel and Divinity are symbiotically linked and, by dint of their ongoing, sweetly coherent intimacies, guarantee life itself. Noting that Nature *is* Spirit manifested, Jung reminds us, "Meaning and purposefulness are not only the prerogatives of the mind; they operate in the whole of living Nature." Fire then is both a physical phenomenon of Nature and also carries enormous cultural and spiri-tual significance. Since the beginning of human history, it has served human societies variously as a primary symbol of the Divine and the spiritually illuminated Self.

Fire can wrap you up in an enchanted mantle turning you and your world upside down, driving you toward the impossible under the most ordinary of circumstances. A symbol of transcendence, it is also stands for our efforts to reach beyond our ordinary selves in order to obtain, even if only for one magically exhilarating moment, the profoundly liberating vision of our own Selves reflected in the eyes of God.

Finally, in its various personified forms as envisioned and experi-enced by each of the sisters, Fire demands a very particular attitudinal approach. In order for the process of individuation or Self-realization to become comprehensible to our rational mind, we are asked to move into a position of conscious surrender. Marie Louise von Franz assures us that "one must simply listen, in order to learn what the in-ner totality—the Self—wants one to do here and now in a particular situation. [And this] impulse comes from the urge toward unique, creative self-realization ... not from the ego, but from the totality of the Spirit: the Self."

Kit's experience reflects this attitude as seen in her email cor-respondence. When she refers to Fire, in most cases, she is referring to the candle flame she keeps alight at all times on her Fire altar in her home. Her meditations and visions are extraordinarily rich and evocative, with the candle flame serving as a living conduit for Fire as

Spirit to enter into the equation.

Entry 1:

Greetings, I just now have time to write to you a bit about my experience with the first meditation you asked us to do, which was to make our intention to participate in the Fire ritual. You asked us to call in the Fire Spirit and ask that it show itself to us. I created my Fire altar at home, and I began with a pink candle. I focused intently on the flame. The sky outside was dark and ominous. I felt very much alone and almost like an abandoned orphan as the wind picked up and the flame began flickering. I was exhausted from work and school and needed to sleep yet had obligations and could not.

I wanted someone to hold and love me as I slept, to handle my obligations. This I brought to my Fire altar and the candle flame and my desire to feel loved, adored, and very much taken care of. The field I work in is draining, and I desperately felt and still feel a need to be nurtured. I feel like I always have to be strong and am often attacked, which is a new experience for me. I lay down after telling the Fire I needed to be loved and cared for. As I admitted my vulnerability to the Fire, I felt sleepier yet felt a strong need to go deep within myself. The pink of the candle then enveloped me in feelings of love and, most importantly, acceptance. I heard a voice telling me that I was different than the norm and that this experience was something I was fully capable of enduring and gracefully embracing. Then I found myself in a vision where I realized that the Fire would be an ally of love, feminine support, passion, and energy. She appeared to me as a flowing, soft, almost pastel-pink pregnant woman in silhouette form.

I was then shown a high roaring river. An image kept reappearing of a log that was damming up a section of the river with leaves and debris preventing the smooth flowing of the water. I asked what the significance of the image was and realized that the physical aches and pains I had in my joints were debris: natural, somewhat toxic debris, compost of a sort that had to be consciously recycled. It was not an artificial toxin that so many accumulate. It could be released as I focused my attention on the pain and asked what its teachings were. This I have yet to do. I then felt my spine elongate and thanked the Spirit of the Fire for the healing.

I also heard in my vision that tilling the soil was a wisdom tradition and a necessity lodged in my bones and that they ached from lack of land connection. I was told that by talking to the land, the plants, animals, and the elements I would begin to heal and in process begin to heal the land as well. She, the land, longs to be spoken to and nurtured, as do I. I have much to explore with this image and work done thus far.

I then heard a raven or crow caw three times and knew I had to pay strict attention to what was to come. I then saw an image of an older man with a pitchfork and farmer jeans with suspenders in my mind's eye. I suspected he had something to do with my ancestors, but I was not sure what. He was definitely a Spirit Helper. Then suddenly, he became a devil calling forth a blazing pitchfork that flew out of my heart. This I have yet to explore. I asked where the ancient Native American warriors were that usually surround me and come to my aid when they are needed, and I heard they were there, paying attention to what was before my eyes.

I realized the message in my vision was that I had to till the soil and feel the dirt. I later tuned in that night and learned more about Plant Spirit Medicine: the ways in which I could serve others through healing that would come through from Tunkashila [Lakota word for grandfather, also meaning Creator] and the Plant Spirits.

Kit describes the Fire in its personified form as "an ally of love, feminine support, passion, and energy" who appears to her "as a flowing, soft, almost pastel-pink pregnant woman in silhouette form." In order to amplify and bring to the forefront our introduction to this enchanting image, I search world religious traditions for a Fire goddess that I could imagine in pastel pink, pregnant with life *in potentia*, tender yet passionately vital, feminine, and with a strong and loving heart. I am drawn irresistibly to the image of Hestia, the wondrous Greek goddess of Fire. As I prepare to "work" Kit's experience, I engage in several conversations with her about Hestia in relation to the marvelous image encountered in her first vision. Her concurrence with my instinctive connection of the two was heart-felt and deeply moving.

Fire as living representative of the Divine was devoutly worshipped in ancient Greece. Even today, a permanent flame is attended to by members of the Greek Orthodox Church in monasteries and chapels intentionally built over ancient pre-Christian sacred sites. Hestia oversees the loving bonds that warm the heart and hearth of a family, a home, and a city. This goddess can fire up a community to create, expand, and flourish or, when necessary, to fiercely protect and defend its borders. In her name, and in the name of other powerful deities, devotees kept the Sacred Fires burning day and night in pristine marble temples and sacred groves throughout ancient Greece. In this way, they guaranteed the constant attention of the gods and goddesses to whom they looked for protection, guidance, loyalty, and love.

Kit's first meditation asks that Fire as Spirit appear by her side. In response, the archetype appears to Kit in personified form as a mother figure: "a flowing, soft, almost pastel-pink pregnant woman." Remember, an archetype, in whatever form it chooses to appear internally, may simultaneously be an autonomous, sacred being external to the individual soul, existing according to its own nature and subject to its own laws, as in the case of a god or a goddess. Arriving at the threshold of Kit's consciousness, this wondrous maternal image by nature draws out Kit's inner child whose image constellates the orphan archetype and related abandonment complex to the surface. Gazing at the candle flame and falling into a deep reverie Kit describes her desperate longing and need to be cared for, to be loved, nurtured, and to be able to rest physically, emotionally and spiritually.

A goddess in her own right, we may also understand Hestia as a mother archetype representing Kit's need to feel safely enclosed and to be taken care of. Kit longs to *be* at home in the deepest sense of that term both inwardly and outwardly. Home is the inner core of her being, where her own centered Self lives yes, but the rest of her is alienated, living on the outside of her own skin, not fitting in, not at home. So it is that, in the silent heart of deep meditation, when Kit invites Fire to show itself to her, it is Hestia's image that appears. From a depth psychological perspective, we may also see the goddess as the personification of an unconscious projection of Kit's own inner need to reclaim and to bring home the orphaned aspect of her own Self.

Let us get to know Hestia. As a rule, it is best not to underestimate the power of any Spirit-charged presence in our field of endeavor. Hestia is at best misunderstood and at worst ignored primarily by male and or male-identified female scholars in the field who undervalue her significance and meaning to the culture and to the Greek pantheon itself. They miss the critically important function across space and time of the feminine values of home and hearth, family loyalty, communal wellbeing, the healing arts, social and charitable imperatives, and fighting to protect their birthright *at all costs*.

As the female aspect of Fire, Hestia as archetype and goddess is both the Source of Life itself and, at the same time, the inner volitional movement of all living things toward their own completion. She is a life cycle, a beautiful and mysterious alchemy unto herself. Hestia is to be found inside the living heart of all things.

Key to knowing how to embrace Hestia into one's life, and to discover the Hestia aspect of one's own Self is this: she is a goddess who *requires* finding. Social psychologist Ginette Paris tells us, "Hestia is the center of the Earth, the center of the home, and her own personal center. She does not leave her place; we must go to her."

A pilgrimage is the requisite means to reach her/your own Fire that fuels the heart-hearth of a home: the safe haven we all need to create, protect, and defend whether in the soul or in our everyday lives. A pilgrimage is a *measured* transformational journey that tasks one with increasingly challenging physical and spiritual responsibilities along the way. This is no easy task as our Fire sister Luna has so eloquently described.

᠉᠉᠉᠉

We all have instilled somewhere deep within us that well-worn cliché, "Home is where the heart is," in fact, it is true, only not at all so simple. What we call home, and all that that brings up in terms of our individual experiences is as powerful and affective a complex as any other.

For our process of Self-discovery to be ultimately successful, it is imperative that we explore each personal complex in the most bravely intimate ways possible as it moves to the forefront of our lived experience. The first thing to face is that we all need to experience "leaving home" not just at some time, but throughout our lives! Life itself will invite, suggest and then force us to forge out, to explore the unknown, and to either conquer or peacefully settle new territory.

For some of us, it may be more about having to abandon home because the notion and the experience of home has caused psychological and emotional damage beyond repair. Others have to escape from home because of the literal danger it poses. Others must leave home forever because of an *inner knowing* that doing so is imperative to realizing their own destiny beyond familial influences and constraints.

That being said, for most of us, the historical reality of home and the lifelong memories it carries for us remains as a living presence throughout our lives, continuing to shape and inform our experiences either as a toxic limitation or as a source of nourishment for the soul. Home is a beautiful, if flawed, complex where a huge piece of our heart is left to serve as a love-sourced homing device for when we find ourselves in critical need of rest and recuperation. When we need to retrace our footsteps carefully, when we need our mothers and fathers, siblings and cousins, when we need to heal in ways that require comfort food prepared lovingly, to breathe in the relaxing fragrances and settle in with the comforting, intimate sounds of familiar surroundings, we simply must go home or create an environment truly reflective of that longing. There is nowhere else that can compare!

And *this* is what Kit desperately yearns for—home, hearth, Mom. Her beautiful vision of Fire as a lovely, pregnant, rose-colored apparition, flowing and pastel, loving and gentle, passionate, brave, and wise, and brilliantly potent with nurturing creative energy describes perfectly the feminine values that ideally represent Kit. Yet, as thinking women know, these are precisely the female attributes that have, for centuries, been the least valued in our histories and cultures. Thus, the contradicted mythologist and classicist, Edith Hamilton, a loyal child of the patriarchal bastion of 20th century British academia, insists on the one hand that Hestia "has no distinct personality and plays *no* [my italics] part in the myths." Yet, in the same breath, she can say, without acknowledgment of the import and significance of her words, that no meal of any kind, *anywhere* in the Greek world could be begun or ended without an offering made to Hestia!

If we consider in ancient times the amount of time and literal manpower that had to be expended every day growing, cultivating, preparing, and eating food, I'm not sure if any other Olympian god or goddess ever warranted that much devoted attention. Hamilton quotes the ancient Greek poet Hesiod's *Hymn to Hestia:*

> Hestia, in all dwellings of men and immortals
> Yours is the highest honor, the sweet wine offered
> First and last at the feast, poured out to you duly.
> Never without you can Gods or mortals hold banquet.

As it is with Hestia, in fact, hearth goddesses all over the world hold "the highest honor." This does not sound to me like a goddess without personality or prestige, let alone without distinction and power in her own right! In fact, in ancient Greece, every city tended a communal sacred hearth in Hestia's name, with *her* Fire being constantly tended upon pain of death! This was considered of such critical importance that if the city Fire-Keeper permitted Hestia's Fire to go out he would be publicly executed. A Greek colony or city could be considered formally established only after the communal Fire hearth to Hestia was built and kindled from coals brought from a neighboring city. These coals needed to have been sourced from *her* Fire altar in that city.

So, *this* also is Kit's Fire spirit, *her* Hestia: a carnelian goddess, melting in the burning heart of the volcano: Earth gestating. She is the wise friend. She is the veiled ancient one "in a small cottage on a hill" who gathers up her Spirit-wisdom over a Sacred Cauldron spilling it into the magical healing potion cooking within.

For me, now caught up in this very same complex as an empathetic witness, Hestia, as with all the spirit beings that grace these pages, represents an aspect of the Divine whose ultimate depths and resources cannot be plumbed. The upwelling of love, guidance, protection, and loyalty, and the immediacy of response to the Self's call for help or, simply for the good company of a divinity, remains the deepest and most beloved of mysteries.

꒰꒰꒱꒱

As we move along the path toward Self-realization, gods and goddesses, and other spirit beings participate in our process will require compensation. These are simply the rules of the game. They may have a task they want us to undertake on their behalf. They may demand hospitality, rituals, and gifts, in other words, a righteous reciprocity fit for beings of their stature. If the Hestia archetype constellates into one's life or manifests as a pattern or complex in one's personal individuation process, as with Kit, unresolved issues surrounding home, family, childhood, and nurturance are often galvanized and brought to the forefront.

In Kit's experience, this is expressed by a deep-seated percolation that surfaces in an upheaval of self-fragmentation, emptiness, and loneliness reflected in her vision of the high, roaring river where a section is dammed by a log and choked with leaves and debris. Asking what the significance of the image is she receives the insight that the recurring, and at times debilitating, pain in her joints is the result, "of debris, natural, somewhat toxic debris, compost of a sort that had to be consciously recycled. It was not," she tells us, "an artificial toxin that so many accumulate. It could be released as I focused my attention on the pain and asked what *its* teachings were."

This is critical to "paying forward" the process of individuation. *Ask* what needs to be done then *do* it. This is what tending to the soul means. It is a lifetime's work. When we are tasked to make the inward move toward a particularly painful issue needing resolution, it is important to remember a fundamental truth: this level of interior repair must often carried out in secret bittersweet solitude in the "dark matter" of the soul.

Interacting with her vision of a clogged and debris-choked river and seeing it as a reflection of her own physical debilitation, Kit admits there is much work to be done. She experiences an immediate visceral response to her statement of willingness to embrace the challenge of change when she says, "I then felt my spine elongate and thanked the Spirit of the Fire for the healing."

Then the vision turns. In the context of soul work one is very often gifted with instructive guidance: a "road map" of understanding, a genealogy of meaning. The voice in Kit's vision, her spirit guide, talks to her about the wisdom traditions contained in the work of tilling the soil. It expands and metaphorically links the basis of the pain in her joints to her lack of connection to the land itself. Here her bones, the structural basis of her physical existence, are literally aching to be tilled, to be "turned over," seeded, and cultivated. Kit is told in her vision that "by talking to the land, the plants, animals, and the elements," she will begin to heal and in the process, "begin to heal the land as well." "She," Kit says, "the land, longs to be spoken to and nurtured, as do I." Here again the *activating* function of symbol, myth, and metaphor emerges. A tiller of soil as both tool and person is, after all, a highly evocative archetypal image.

Remember that these are also self-aspects of Kit's own being. Kit as tiller of her own *ground of being* and, by extension, the ground of Earth herself, is a powerful image. I imagine a shining, green, rural landscape where industrious life-generating work is being done under a watchful blue sky by a simple, hardworking soul at peace with her known world and with herself. To take this metaphor further, a tiller is also a tool used to prepare hardened soil for planting by breaking it up and incorporating organic material into it thus transforming it into soft, freshly turned, and fertile soil. We know that the soul too requires constant and careful turning and tending like the best of gardens and meadows so it can produce everything our lives could ever need. For Kit, like crystal, the inspiration is clear. "I realized," she says, "the message in my vision was that I had to till the soil and feel the dirt."

Kit's vision of where she needs to direct her ongoing path toward becoming a healer comes into play again when she shares, "I later tuned in that night and learned more about Plant Spirit Medicine; the ways in which I could serve others through healing that would come through from *Tunkashila*, and the Plant Spirits." *Tunkashila* is the Lakota Sioux word for grandfather or Creator. Kit is speaking of studying with shamanic teachers who work with plants as spirit beings. This wisdom tradition is something that human communities relied on for millennia along with the medicinal remedies produced from the natural world. Tribal communities worldwide continue with these traditional healing modalities even today.

There is an important lesson here for us all. In order for our species to survive, we must begin to function actively with all living beings as family, as *actual* relatives who are coequal in value, significance, and importance as our human relations are. From this perspective, we can begin to understand how ancient and present day indigenous communities have lived together *with* plants, accepting their generous offerings of food, shelter, warmth, and healing medicines offering in return protection, tending and cultivation.

Today, we have created a vast science of healing substances taken from plant life, often at the expense of those very same plants, but we have forgotten that, as spirit beings, plants also can assist in healing, harmonizing, and balancing our own lives at the level of soul. This is the path that Kit has been guided to take as part of her own journey toward knowing her Self as a healer and discovering the Divine in a new dimension.

ＪＪＪ

But, the path toward the Self and wholeness, as we have already seen with our poetess Luna, is strewn with obstacles and trickery. There is just no way around it. In the same vision, hearing a raven caw three times Kit understands that she is to be attentive and on guard. This is important. There is magic afoot.

From earliest times through to the modern period among tribal communities and among people who have rediscovered and now respect and revere these old ways, Raven is understood to be a powerful spirit being. Raven is a complex. He is a transcendent symbol, the archetype of ordered chaos, change, and the imperative of creation itself. He is the creator of Earth, Sun, Moon, Fire, and of the Star Nations. He is also the benevolent provider of food and fresh water for his human creation.

But, Raven is also a dualistic personality. He can be a dangerous trickster playing incomprehensible and often cruel tricks on an unsuspecting soul. With the trickster archetype, you had better be on your toes, know *what* or *who* is really in front of you, and be ready to run, hide or, if you are confident of the win, stand your ground. Raven is also a spirit being of the highest order that serves as mediator and messenger between life and death, between experiencing ordinary life on this earth and life in the realm of the Sacred. In this respect, he oversees the actions of men in war, their dying and transition to the afterworld, and teaches the wisdom traditions surrounding the burial of the dead and the subsequent journeying of the soul into the next life.

Kit's inner needs as they are articulating in her visions have drawn an extraordinary presence into her life in the form of Raven. To enrich the moment even further, Raven caws three times. Raven speaks. Kit must be able to *listen* to and *understand* the message, but knowing the language of birds is a gift from the Divine and petitions must be made, offerings gifted and a commitment made to learning the art and the craft involved. Maybe not right now, but if Raven is to accompany Kit on her life's passage she will need to make these requests knowing the sacrifice involved.

In Norse mythology, the power to understand the language of the birds is a sign of great wisdom. The blind god Odin has two ravens serving as his eyes and ears, who fly great distances to observe what people are doing and report back to their great Lord. In ancient times, goddess Athena gifted the Greek prophet Tiresias with the ability to understand the language of the birds. In the mystical traditions of the Kabbalah in Judaism and Sufism in Islam, the language of birds is considered to be the secret language of angels and holds the key to perfect knowledge.

Raven speaks to Kit three times. What is the significance of the number three? What does it mean? According to St. Augustine, who lived in the 4th century C.E., numbers represent a revealed sacred language and all created things are in numerical relationship to each other. He insists that it is up to us to search and discover the secrets of these relationships or petition God to reveal them to us. What a wonder! Raven is perched and, *because* he is talking in threes, Kit *understands* instinctively that she is to be on her guard and to pay attention to what is coming next.

And rightfully so because just at this moment, another image appears. It is an older man wearing farmer's jeans with suspenders and carrying a pitchfork. Shaken to the core, Kit tells us, "I suspected he had something to do with my ancestors but I was not sure what." This farmer image appears as a duality. He has a benign and safe persona to begin with; a salt-of-the-earth kind of man, an American farmer, or maybe an ancestor. He is definitely a spirit helper as Kit assures us in all confidence.

Certainly farmer is a pivotal, archetypal entity. To start with, he is a god figure like Osiris in ancient Egypt, who was the first farmer. He taught his people farming techniques and the domestication of animals. Farmer is also the provider of a "way station" for deities, angels, seekers of soul, and ordinary travelers alike. He is a player in fate and destiny and is a messenger for kings, queens, gods, and goddesses alike.

But, remember that Raven as trickster is present too and just as Kit is beginning to feel safe and on familiar ground with the farmer, he suddenly becomes a devil who extracts a blazing pitchfork out of her heart. It is such a frightening and contradicted image that she stands down from the effort to comprehend, telling herself instead, "this I have yet to explore" all the while looking around in her vision for the ancient Native American warriors who have been her protectors and guardians in spirit for several years. In fact, they are present but stand only as silent, passive witnesses to her experience. Sometimes we must make the journey utterly alone.

Entry 2:

Greetings, please forgive for not writing sooner. I have been busy and yet have a dear and wise friend in Fire. Thank you for inviting me to participate in the Fire ritual. I feel honored. Please pardon the raw phraseology.

About 3 weeks ago, at my altar, I told the Fire I would be bringing a glass heart to the Ritual. The Fire accepted the gift, and I suddenly felt sad and a deep sense of loneliness came over me. I felt crowded with memories and wanted to cry, if not wail, but could not. I felt stuck and far from my inner self. Actually, I am feeling that way again. I feel out of synch with the institutions I am involved with: school and work.

I am also uncomfortable with Rain Child, which is

challenging, as I have been doing sweat lodges for about a year now. Her ways are different from mine, and so I am quiet and want to be left alone and respected for the ways I have been taught. I am not interested in being forced to follow ways that are uncomfortable or strange to me. It is not a big deal, but I have been feeling raw and want a safe place for my spiritual practice. I know that when one door closes, another opens. I'll just see what comes next.

Anyway, back to the topic at hand. I focused on the candle flame at my Fire altar and gently, slowly knew that I had to bring my centered, strong, real self to the Fire. There at my altar, the message coming from the Fire was clear, direct, and unwavering. I am still searching for her, the centered self, and feel ripped apart at the moment. I am not yet getting a symbol or guidance as to what to bring to the ritual, yet as I write this, the tears are beginning to flow. Possibly at work tonight, they'll come. I explained to the Fire that my schedule does not allow me to get the social nurturing I am used to, as I am a social being. I need the balance of solitude and interactions of depth. I suspect that once I start being present with the pain and tears, the image will present itself. I know more shall be revealed. Much Love. Kit.

[Author's note: The sweat lodge is one of the Seven Sacred Rites of the Sioux tribes and will be described in greater detail in a later section.]

In exchange for the gift of Hestia's guiding, comforting, healing, and fiercely protective presence, the goddess invites us to bring ourselves into alignment with her own divine nature in all its centrifugal, fiery energy. It is a radiant force expressed in her guardianship of family, safety, security, and her love of peace and harmony. At the same time, if necessary, she can run amok wreaking havoc wherever she touches down. If we are unable to resource and commune with our actual flesh and blood family, Hestia guides us to create a home and hearth and a family in spirit. This may be an inner, sacredly-sourced community within our own selves functioning at the level of soul where our own Eternal Fire resides; and or an outer community of dear friends whose closeness and active loving serve as a beautiful replacement to one's flesh and blood ties.

To realize and experience ourselves as whole and complete human beings we must live simultaneously as both solitary and communal beings. Kit is searching for this balance. And, contrary to the fundamental purpose of her Lakota spiritual practices, which involve the creating and sustaining of a familial community, a *tiochpaye*, the spiritual leader of Kit's community is creating an environment of conflict, discomfort, and alienation for her.

Meditating at her Fire altar and focusing intently on the candle flame, Kit cries, "I am still searching for her, the centered Self, and feel ripped apart at the moment … as I write this, the tears are beginning to flow … I need the balance of solitude and interactions of depth." She is now fully caught up in her orphan complex.

"To have a family life that warms us," Ginnette Paris tells us, "we must, as with the flame of Hestia, maintain it, watch over it, nourish it, and place it at the center of our attention." Kit must do this for her Self *and* for the Fire goddess precisely because her personal invocation to Fire has called forth a spirit of that caliber! She is required to *host* her special guest accordingly so that *both* are nourished and kept alive by the life-sustaining force of Fire. Goddess and mortal woman are equally responsible to themselves and to each other for keeping the Eternal Flame burning within and without. Remember the fate of the neglectful ancient Fire Keeper who allowed the Sacred Fire to go out. Remember Luna's story.

Entry 3:

Greetings, a friend just came over to my house and gave me an acupuncture treatment. She discovered that I had a lot of heat trapped within my body. As I relaxed into a deep dream state, I felt the heat arise from my belly and felt like I was in the heart of a volcano about to explode. I sensed that I was to listen to the story behind this heat.

The Fire was orange, and I suddenly saw that it was burning in a hut somewhere in the mountains with a cloaked figure brewing herbs over its flames in a cauldron of sorts. A Hearth, heart, and I remembered that hearts have traditionally been the center of home. I suspected this woman was brewing a healing, somewhat-magical potion that was considered folk medicine in another time and place, possibly Europe. My ancestors come from the highlands of Scotland and that may be the location, but it is a guess, a hunch of some sort.

I then dreamt that I was somewhere in the mountains of South America learning how to prepare herbs that release heat in a safe way. This may have something to do with the transformative nature of Fire. This is becoming quite a journey, one I did not expect. I am learning much about my process in life, and the Fire, even during these weeks of preparing for the Ritual, is beginning to transform and move the inner stagnation. I'll keep you posted. It could be that I am to bring a specific herb to the Fire ritual? More shall be revealed. Much Love. Kit.

Let us now gaze on this Fire goddess from a different vantage point as we scan the panorama of Kit's own vision and situate it in an even more complex world of broader meaning. As in the time of ancient Greece and Rome, today we know that Earth's central core is Fire, the place from which she continuously gives birth to and nourishes her own physical body. Earth, in her Hestia aspect, has both a molten, free-flowing lava core and a "womb" or hearth in which to house it.

Ancient Mediterranean cultures envisioned Earth's hearth as an *omphalos*, which can be described as Fire encased in soil or clay. Humans over the centuries have built clay ovens where radiant heat cooks food and heats indoor and outdoor environments. In an *omphalos*, hot embers can also be preserved indefinitely until needed. Modern geologists confirm that the center of the Earth is actually Fire encased by surface ground. As we cultivate ourselves into soulful,

Self-aware, generative, compassionate, and creative humans, we need to take care of the Fire of life within our own beings, making sure we build an efficient and safe *omphalos* of the soul from well-fired "clay" formed out of the vicissitudes of our own life experiences.

It is this explosive Hestia, this dangerously unpredictable volcanic being, lava flowing in her guts, this cauldron-tending, bewitching deity that comes to mind when Kit describes the Spirit-sourced instructions arising from the "heat in her belly" and from the "heart of the volcano" that urge her to "listen to the story behind this heat." Suddenly, she is transported in her vision to an ancient place in an ancient time, possibly the Scottish Highlands, the birthplace of her ancestors, where she sees a Fire burning inside a small hut nestled against a mountainside.

An enigmatic, cloaked female figure is inside the hut hunched over a steaming cauldron brewing a healing, magical concoction. The cloak, implying the existence of a mystery, at once adds depth to the scenario. Jung describes these kinds of historical associations as "the link between the rational world of consciousness and the world of instinct. Associations and images of this kind," he says, "are an integral part of the soul, and can be observed everywhere. They are not in any sense lifeless or meaningless 'remnants.' They still function, and they are especially valuable." Kit correctly intuits that these symbolic images are conveying the dynamic nature of Fire in her own process of individuation.

Let's discuss the image and feeling-tone of a "volcano about to explode." This kind of phrase represents an initiatory position of the Self when it is on the edge of things and ready to make a transformative move. The tension in this position is that it elicits the ego-personality to take up a correspondingly resistant position with an equivalent strength of heart. Here's the key. The ego does not appreciate change, to put it mildly, and will not budge without a fight. But the victory in the making is beautiful if one's courage holds.

The image of a volcano as archetypal symbol has a highly effective operational function in the human soul. It is a critical function,

THE FLAME

without which most seeking souls would flounder and disappear in a spiral of timid, impotent encounters.

The word *volcano* comes from the Latin *volcanus*. The great Roman God of Fire is Vulcan, also known as Hephaestus to the ancient Greeks. Now Hephaestus is important to this discussion for he is the male counterpart to Hestia. Like Shiva to his own Shakti, and Freyja to her Freya, we may say that Hephaestus *is* Hestia in male. Remember, as Kit prepares for her own Fire ritual, equally prominent male and female forces appear in her visions proving integral to her Self-identity.

Hephaestus is orphaned as a child by his mother, the goddesses Hera, who, on seeing that he was born lame, cast him out of Mount Olympus to live abandoned and alone on the tiny Greek island of Lemnos. You see, Hestia in her male aspect also suffers from an orphan complex.

On his eventual return to Mt. Olympus, Hephaestus is tasked with tending to the Original Fire and overseeing the Divine Armory of the Gods. Yet, at another level, like his beloved twin Hestia, Hephaestus is a kind and peace-loving god, a protector of children, and a guardian and sustainer of human civilization. For without the White Fire of the Sacred Forge, without the Golden Fire of the Hearth, without the Red Fire in Earth's own molten womb, without the Black Fire of the Thunderbolt, and without a righteous god or goddess to tend to them, there would be no life at all.

Kit's vision resonates with the power embodied in the metaphor of the volcano. It is a transcendent symbol operating in Kit's life and imaged by her as a terrific "heat in her belly." We may also understand the volcano as Earth's "uterine" self that functions at precise moments in time just as a woman's menstrual cycle does. In rivulets of blood, and according to the draw of the moon, a woman sloughs off the inner lining of her uterus every month only to immediately begin preparing again for the conception of a new life. And believe me, there is heat involved! So too, Earth reveals her inner molten core, spilling red rivers of liquid Fire up and out onto the surface of her own body either to cleanse, rejuvenate, and build up her own fertile skin or to give birth to herself. We can witness this breathtaking sight on the Big Island of Hawaii. Night and day, day and night, at land's edge, a lava-fall of golden, flowing coils tumbles into the cool blue embrace of the salty Pacific. Wherever there is a great birthing going on, whether on Earth's own body or within our own human souls, representatives of the Divine will gather and make themselves known, if invited.

Volcano as archetype also represents a threshold experience, either as a place, or as a moment in time through which one moves from the darkest depths into the conscious light of day, crossing boundaries, seeing things from another vantage point. Depending on the situation or circumstance, negotiating a threshold encounter can be a violent and eruptive experience. Emotional or physical wounds repressed in silent suffering fester over time, causing in the process a meltdown that ultimately settles into a Fire of rage. Over time, these burning, pent-up energies explode onto the surface of things in an intensity of emotionally charged perceptions that may lead to irrational and sometimes destructive decisions resulting in regrettable actions.

Kit feels this "volcanic explosion" as imminent in her life. Although she is reluctant and fearful, in her own words, "to let it erupt," she is also aware that allowing the fury to detonate at this time might be an ultimately creative act, moving her toward the Self-transformation she yearns for.

Reflectively understood, in order for Earth to re-create herself in perpetuity, she needs to *necessarily* create what we often interpret as a path of tragic devastation leading ultimately to new life. This is one of those terrible beauties we must face with humility, understanding our rightful and relatively insignificant place in *her* greater scheme of things.

From the standpoint of the human soul, an eruption of emotionally charged repressed content frequently manifests first in anger. When left unchecked, this emotion is difficult to contain let alone channel constructively, yet this is precisely what an individual must do in order to balance its potentially destructive effects on relationships, career, one's own person, and on the quality and meaning of life itself. Our task is to set in place an internal system of psychological and emotional checks and balances so that no matter the situation or circumstance, no matter the stresses and strains involved, our internal equilibrium is not compromised.

When a particularly powerful archetype such as goddess Hestia is constellated in one's life, we are obligated to note the precise checks and balances or "self-regulations" that are consequently set into motion explicitly in relation to that particular sacred presence. In Kit's actual and visionary experience the increasingly disturbing sense of a volcano preparing to explode in her belly is counteracted by the image of a small, secure little cottage in which a mysterious, yet somehow known, female figure is creating a magical potion in a cauldron over a blazing, yet *contained*, Fire.

Along with Kit, we may understand this image as the Hestia aspect within our own Selves. Actively engaged in the alchemical work of "cooking" things up, this archaic woman, mantled in mystery, invites a sense of timelessness, of the arcane, and of necessarily secret mysteries as she creates a spellbinding substance in a magical cauldron forged from eternal possibilities. For Kit, the cauldron represents both the source and container wherein her life is continually being conceived, gestated, and translated into her future. She becomes witness to her own archaic Self, called up from the depths of her own being, busy in the small cottage clinging to the mountainside, cooking up her own life's destiny.

Kit must reclaim and renovate certain aspects of her Self in the most formal terms if she is to remain within Hestia's gravitational pull and benefit from this great goddess's presence in her life. We could say that she is being invited to contribute to her own individuation process by serving as a *binding factor* to the inner complex of relationships between all aspects of herself that are hard at work at this time. She must become an agent of love, enhanced in flavor by delicious sensitivities and deeper intimacies that, like herbs and spices, make any meal a meal to remember.

In the midst of her *nigredo*, her own dark night of the soul, but with Hestia as her ally, it becomes unnecessary for Kit to experience the impending violent eruption of her pent-up frustrations, hurts, disappointments, betrayals, and despair. Her/Hestia's cauldron has become the "pressure cooker" required to carefully detoxify all those aspects of her Self in need of an alchemy: an authentic process of transformation leading to permanent change. Rather than emerging at will as toxic flows of anger, grief, and pain welling up from the depths, these pressure-cooked fragments are instead reconstituted as nutrients for the soul and building blocks for the evolving Self.

Hestia has called Kit to join her. It is a call sent directly to Kit's wild and unbounded Self who is able to journey in vision into the world of Spirit. Kit must reclaim those aspects of her Self named Woman of the Hearth and Wise Woman of the Cauldron, both in the outer world and within her own soul. We need to keep our homes, our lives, and our soul-referenced Selves in order by both literally and metaphorically cleaning, washing, cooking, tidying, planning, and contributing depth and meaning. Clarissa Pinkola-Estes puts it this way: "Most of us would do better if we became more adept at watching Fire; watching more closely the cooking process for nourishing the wild Self. Too often we turn away from the pot, from the oven. We forget to watch, forget to add fuel, and forget to stir the pot. So, it is the cooking up of new things, of new directions, of commitments to one's art and work that continuously nourishes the wild soul. Without the Fire, our great ideas, our original thoughts, our yearnings and longings remain uncooked and everyone is unfulfilled."

Entry 4:

> *Greetings, thank you, thank you for a healing journey during this last weekend's Fire ritual. I'm looking forward to more and have been experiencing a deepening of the feminine. And*

now that it is over and I continue with the practice. I stare into the Fire inside the tiny pink candle flame, comfortably basking in my living room in the warmth of the sun's Fire. I glance out the window and see a hawk circling counter clockwise high in the sky and feel the familiar, immediate confirmation of why Hawk Wing will accompany me on my spirit journeys from now on. I am made aware that its talons are now pulling out of my heart, my very being, what is no longer useful and what holds me back from being, simply being, BEING all that I have been, am, and will be in the light of this woman who is me, KIT SANTORINI. As I breathe, the candle flame flickers and I remember the intimate connection I share with the Tate [Lakota for Wind)]: my relative the wind that communicates what is often unknown to the naked eye and is also known as a form of intuition.

The still flame and yellow candle at my Fire altar allows me to observe and inwardly dance the Dance of Wind and Fire. As I do so, Shadows of the leaves outside my window beckon, calling me to enter into their Mysteries. To know as medicine the gifts they bring to a cauldron of brewing herbs simmering over the Hearth Fire; medicine/food that wants to deeply connect with all that is and to be transformed in the consuming and the healing. The very act of my awareness of plants' presences speaks volumes and I am suddenly reminded of the sweet morning kisses of my cat earlier this morning as I rested and he nestled close to me, silky fur rubbing up against my cheek in a moment of loving connection. The bushes reeling now from the fierce wind and rain again knock on the window. Where this is leading to is so deep, deeper, and again ever so deep within.

Crazy Horse, Chief Joseph, and Geronimo, I call upon them in my prayers for transformation. I am told they will give me a song as a sign that I am to remember the fierceness of the wind and rain (air and water) that completes the transformation begun by the Fire: sun's internal generator; the warmth that reaches far and wide; touches all and does not discriminate. I sense that Crazy Horse transformed loneliness and exhaustion into a way of being that embodied an inner knowingness we all search for in the divine service of self and others.

The state of busyness/shallow mind and seemingly shallow/hallow interactions are then deepened; again deep into the Self and through the breath of Fire continually changing and transforming at times through the Fire of Dragon Breath and sometimes through the gentle orange/yellow still flame that accompanies me into the sweet embrace of the elements, of original being, of Fire, heart and into myself. Much Love. Kit.

After the Fire ritual is over some several days later, Kit shares, "I continue with the practice. I stare into the Fire inside the tiny pink candle flame, comfortably basking in my living room in the warmth of the sun's Fire."

In her first meditation with the candle flame after the Fire ritual, Kit glances out of the window and glimpses a hawk circling counter clockwise high in the sky. Hawk is a great and noble beauty, serving symbolically as a messenger for the Divine. As a powerful transformational symbol, when Hawk appears in your life you are being invited to explore and question your views. Hawk is asking you to consider the depth and breadth of your vision. Are you seeing things clearly? Are you accurately perceiving the reality, the authenticity, or truth of a given situation or circumstance? Are you able to move to higher ground in your thinking and observation of things too close at hand? Do you need to become more keenly aware of something? Listen to Hawk's piercing cry. Pay attention. The message may be a wonderful one.

For Kit, it is a bittersweet boon of the highest merit in symbolic terms. In the glimpse of the hawk circling overhead outside her window, she receives an important insight: "Hawk Wing will accompany me on my spirit journeys from now on." The sweetness of the gift lies simply in being included in the gracious company of this totemic spirit being.

The bitter brew lies in the suffering while peeling off layers of negative residuals. What are these residuals? They appear in the form of lifelong patterns of self-criticism, self-judgment, self-diminishing responses to life's vicissitudes, and the lack of courage of conviction grounded in love. Inviting Hawk into her life as a change agent of the soul, Kit laments, "I am made aware that its talons are now pulling out of my heart, my very being, what is no longer useful and what holds me back from being, simply being, BEING all that I have been, am, and will be in the light of this woman who is me, KIT SANTORINI."

Kit's vision shifts inward now, guided by the still flame of the yellow candle at her Fire altar. It invites her to embrace and "inwardly dance the Dance of Wind and Fire." Again, earlier visions that have left their mark reappear on the surface of things. As the leaves of trees and bushes begin to rustle outside her window, she hears their personal invitation to "enter into their Mysteries." Images of plants and the spirits they embody come into view as they offer the gift of knowledge about their healing abilities. She sees this in very real connection now with the cauldron of healing herbs "simmering over the Hearth Fire" inside the ancient cottage on the hillside where her ancestors once roamed.

Her insight deepens as she describes, "medicine/food that wants to deeply connect with all that is and to be transformed in the consuming and the healing. The bushes reeling now from the fierce wind and rain again knock on the window. Where this is leading to is so deep, deeper, and again ever so deep within." Kit's heartfelt cry for guidance on how to discover and develop her own contribution to this world, her longing for a deepening of her soul-centered Self, and her wish to connect authentically with family and a community are all being addressed here.

Kit then calls on Crazy Horse of the Oglala Sioux, Chief Joseph of the Nez Perce, and Geronimo of the Chiricahua Apache. Like her Fire sisters, Kit is a fighter, advocate, rebel, and protagonist for change. Her companions in the world of Spirit include these great warriors who, though vanquished, have left a legacy of standing strong in their own truth. Their spirits still roam free and wild, wise like the four winds. With their spirits nearby, Kit is "signed" to call on them in her "prayers of transformation for all those that suffer and for a release of bondage."

They also appear bringing gifts as all true boon companions do. For Kit, it will be a song of power, singing the "fierceness of the wind and rain (air and water) that completes the transformation begun by the Fire, sun's internal generator; the warmth that reaches far and wide; touches all and does not discriminate." This insight is even more profound for those who walk a solitary path through their own personal wilderness: "I sense," Kit tells us, "that Crazy Horse transformed loneliness and exhaustion into a way of being that embodied an inner knowingness we all search for."

What follows is the continuing resonance for Kit around the Fire ritual at Indian Canyon, particularly in the context of her participation in Native American spiritual practices.

Entry 5:

Greetings. Over these past few weeks of preparing for and participating in the Fire ritual, I have learned new ways to be with and to communicate with Fire inwardly and outwardly. And it has affected me deeply as well as been a wonderful gift from Spirit.

This weekend at a sweat lodge ceremony, I spent some time with the Fire and want to share my discoveries. It is about how the Fire work that we did together during the Fire rite is continuing. I was going to bring in the stones and tend the Fire for the ceremony and suddenly, confronted by the intense heat of the looming Fire and its flames, I felt frail and intimated. I could feel its intensity begin to burn off shreds of falsehoods and secrets that I had hidden so deeply within that

I was unaware of their insidious nature. I knew at that moment I would be forever changed after this ceremony working with the Fire.

I had not expected to encounter such heat and a feeling of nakedness before the spirit of this Fire as it kept building and continued to grow and spread its heat. I felt taunted by the flame's wild nature and erratic movements. The Fire danced with the fierce winds and menacing dark clouds overhead. It felt like all of nature was conspiring to pull out all pretensions. Hawks circled above as if waiting to attack their prey and coyotes yapped in the distance, seeming to mock my vulnerability. I stepped away from the Fire to greet friends who had arrived to participate in the ceremony. I shivered uncontrollably with a sense of dread. Something was rattled within and, I thought, horribly amiss.

I then felt enveloped in a fog and fell into a time warp of sorts. The air became unusually and yes, eerily still, and I focused on my prayers. Suddenly, the Fire then died down somewhat and became easily accessible. I stared into the Fire searching for guidance before entering the womb of the mother and sensed that the Spirit of the Fire was letting me know it would be gentle as I was to grow and learn in a new way from this moment forward. We then entered the sweat lodge, shared sacred words, and I prepared myself to bring in the stones. After the first round of the ceremony was concluded, I crawled out of the lodge to tend the Fire and prepare to bring more rocks into the Lodge. The flames had miraculously died down, and I was able to work much more closely with the Fire. In the second round, inside the lodge, I heard myself pray asking that everything preventing me from being close to the Creator be removed. This was not a conscious prayer; it simply appeared or evolved out of my own depths.

I felt like a tree in the center of a Medicine Wheel with its roots deeply imbedded within Mother Earth and its branches

*reaching high into the now starlit sky. The stones were talking
inside the lodge. I looked intently at each one and saw many
ancient faces gazing back at me that I sensed had walked
with me for eternity. I had no real conception of time; it felt
timeless. Struggling to see the stone's faces, they disappeared
and then not remembering how, I crawled out at the end of
the ceremony. Then I was suddenly out under the night sky
looking into the smoldering embers of the ceremonial Fire,
and in my mind's eye, I saw buffalo being slaughtered. I felt
temporarily disoriented and quickly regained my composure,
promising myself to journey within and learn more about this
image that came from the Fire. I had to socialize with dear
friends after the sweat lodge and lost some of the altered state
that allowed me to perceive another level of reality. More shall
be revealed Ismana. I have been busy and hope to continue
the journey with the Fire today. Much Love. Kit.*

There is a profound continuity of experience after the Fire ritual
in Indian Canyon, almost a concluding rite of passage that needs to
translate for Kit in another cultural world: that of her involvement with
the indigenous spirituality of the Lakota Sioux. After the Fire ritual at
Indian Canyon, she is invited to tend the Sacred Fire for a women's
sweat lodge ceremony, a responsibility she has never formally taken
on before. She moves from a deeply personal sequence of visions
where one of the primary images is that of the small ancestral cottage
hidden in the mountain fastness in which a solitary Cloaked Woman
ritually tends to the Sacred Fire and to a Cauldron filled with spiritual
potency and a prophetic future. Now, in the bright light of day, she is
given the opportunity to realize her longings for family, love, and a
true sense of belonging that may be experienced as a part of a Native
American ceremonial circle.

In *The Sacred Pipe*, the holy man, Black Elk, of the Oglala Sioux,
shares the spiritual traditions of his people in moving and inspired
terms. In the language of "the people," this tremendously beautiful rite

is called *Inipi* meaning purification ceremony. In English, it is known as sweat lodge. It is a *Wakan,* or holy activity, offered to *Wakan Tanka,* the Great Spirit, the Creator, the Source and Sustainer of all life.

The many ritual processes involved in the *Inipi* together represent all the "powers" of the created universe and are invoked with prayers and sacred songs while, at the same time, being incorporated as individual living spirits into every aspect of the ritual. *"O Wakan Tanka I shall build the sacred path of life. By purifying ourselves for the people, we shall walk this path with firm steps for it is the path leading to you. May my people walk this path! May we be pure! May we live again!"* Black elk.

The *Inipi* is built on sanctified ground, usually in a private and protected area encircled by trees, hidden in a canyon, or nestled in the bank of a creek or small rivulet. It is woven out of sixteen flexible willow branches, one of which signifies the presence of *Wakan Tanka,* and in that capacity serves as the "key" or a threshold that opens the doorway to the created universe, to the Spirit World. It is a humble, basket-like structure dug into the bare earth, as pliable as the sixteen silver-green willows sacrificed to frame it.

A small, circular depression in the center of the *Inipi* is dug out and dedicated with prayer and song, becoming symbolically the Center of the Universe. It is an altar inviting the presence of *Wakan Tanka*. It also serves as "home and hearth" for the twenty-eight or more *Inyan Wakan,* sacred rocks that have been heated in the *Peta Owihankeshni,* the Eternal Fire. While signifying the eternal and imperishable nature of the Great Spirit, these sacred *Inyans* also represent the *Ina Maka,* Earth Mother, or *Unchi Maka,* Grandmother Earth, from whom all life-sustaining constituents are gifted to every living thing. The sweat lodge is often referred to as the womb of Earth Mother. *"Hau! Ina Maka, Unchi Maka, you are Wakan and listen to our prayers sacredly; hear me! We have come from you, we are a part of you, and we know that our bodies will return to you at that time when our spirits travel upon the great path; I remember YOU to whom my body will return."* Black Elk.

The *Inipi* rites begin with building the Fire in the sacred area a few feet from the sacred lodge. Before lighting the wood, prayers and songs are sent to *Wakan Tanka* asking that He, in his spirit form, as *Peta Owihankeshni*, Eternal Fire, enter into the flames. *"O Wakan Tanka, this is your eternal Fire that has been given to us on this great island! It is your will that we build this place in a sacred manner. The eternal Fire always burns, through it we shall live again by being made pure and by coming closer to your powers."* Black Elk.

Just before the *Inipi* is to begin, the lodge is covered with several layers of blankets or cloth tarps so that it becomes pitch black inside. The participants crawl inside and sit silently around the rock pit while the leader of the *Inipi*, sometimes called the Water Pourer, begins the ceremony. Prayers are said and songs sung in ritual order while the heated rocks, sometimes also referred to as the Ancestors are brought into the lodge.

Water is poured on the rocks and hot steam representing the Sacred Breath rises creating a shock of heat that causes the participants to sweat profusely thus becoming purified in body, mind, and spirit. *"O ancient rocks, you are now here with us with your sacred breath; Wakan Tanka has made the Earth, and has placed you next to her. Upon you generations will walk and their steps shall not falter."* Black Elk.

For the most part, indigenous rituals across the world, by their very nature, can pose grave dangers to the naïve, to the uninitiated, and to the seeker simply dabbling for the next spiritual high. Kit is invited to interact with Fire in a manner and at a level of responsibility unlike any she has known before in her participation in the *Inipi*. This is a profound postscript to her experience with Fire in the company of her Fire Sisters.

At the same time, the invitation to serve as Fire Keeper for the *Inipi* powerful counterpoint to the vision of her Self, identified as the ancient Cloaked Woman alone at the Hearth Fire, alone with her Cauldron. Now, she is being called out to work with Fire elementally on its own terms out on the land. Its nature will be determined by the air, the wind, the temper of the surroundings, and the way in which she tends to it on a visceral, intuitive, and conscious level.

She will be responsible to the Water Pourer for maintaining not only the spiritual depth and integrity, the *Wakan,* of the ritual from the standpoint of Fire but also for the safety of the participants who are her spiritual family. She must also keep the surrounding environment and herself safe. Remember, Fire untended is a force of destruction in the making.

Once the sacred *Inyans* have been stacked on the wood and the *Peta Owihankeshni* is lit all senses and inner knowing must come into play for the Fire Keeper. It is a large Fire that exerts the most intense heat. It may burn for several hours with the heat needing to be maintained at the highest levels. Fire Keepers are often in dangerously close physical contact with the flames. Only the gentleness and care, the honesty and purity of heart and mind, a steadfast courage, and again, the love we bear for Earth and for Spirit keeps us safe.

Relationally, the *Inyans* being brought to life in the heart of Fire's blaze also require constant acknowledgment and care as they transform into spirits. If one does not treat these "rock people" with the proper degree of formality and care they can also cause great harm.

Kit finds the courage to accept the invitation to take on the duties and responsibilities of Fire Keeping, even though she freely admits that she is afraid and tentative. Her fears are well grounded since she does undergo a severe testing, both physically and from the point of view of her own Self's individuation, as she works with Fire. You see, she knows that having accepted the honor of being a Fire Keeper for the *Inipi* there is no changing her mind. In spite of her fear, she is going to have to surrender to Fire, asking for its protection in order to remain safe in the tending.

As she endures the painful intensity of the heat Kit begins to experience the "shreds of falsehoods and secrets, insidious in nature," that she has buried "so deeply within" being burned off her. She understands that in order to remain unharmed she must willingly enter into a state of oneness with Fire the way a woman does when faced with an enchanting and incandescent beauty, moving in a rapture of love.

When we offer our soul-referenced Self over to a great archetype, a god or goddess, or in this case, the Great Spirit, *Wakan Tanka*, we are propelled headlong into a position of truth. "I had not expected," Kit said, "to encounter such heat and a feeling of nakedness before the spirit of this Fire."

Kit has moved into a reflective attitude with regard to her fear of Fire and her own relationship to that fear. She begins to question the conscious process of dealing with her fear while at the same time acknowledging the depth of her reverence and love of Fire. She remembers how it manifested itself to her in so many stirring images, communicating and working with her on so many levels throughout the past few weeks leading up to and during the Fire ritual.

Fear and love converging reveal the insidious actions of our false self-perceptions. Marie von Franz calls this is "a living insight which is the bitter truth." Even more importantly, this living insight becomes a transformative truth that Kit recognizes. "I knew at that moment," she says, "I would be forever changed after this ceremony and working with the Fire."

I can say from personal experience that the *Peta Owihankeshni* and its requirements of those who tend to it allow for no half measures. It will pit you against yourself, put you through your paces and will brook no doubt or uncertainty in its unrelenting demands for constant and exclusive attention. It's just how Spirit works. It's all or nothing.

In Kit's case, it is after the fear is resolved, after she has received a visionary insight, and only after her whole persona has been jolted, questioned, and revealed to be fraught with serious flaws, that a transitional moment occurs and she can at last find her ease with the Fire.

This encounter with Fire at the *Inipi* after the Fire ritual at Indian Canyon illustrates vividly that Fire has now become a prime mover in Kit's life. Her visionary experience shows Fire as a multifaceted, transformational symbol and, for those of us who choose to see things in this way, a powerful, autonomous force in its own right. Imaged as a gentle, loving, nurturing, pregnant woman, it represents the nurturing heart and soul of home and hearth. As a timeless force, it transports Kit to an ancient, ancestral time where her archaic Self, symbolized by the Cloaked Woman works with the spirits of medicinal plants combining them together to form healing remedies.

Fire also provides Kit a threshold experience through which she may forge out on journeys into other worlds. It is also the dragon's breath that gifts those brave enough to come near. In her own words, "The state of busyness/shallow mind and seemingly shallow/hallow interactions are then deepened; again deep into the Self, and through the breath of Fire, continually changing and transforming, at times through the Fire of Dragon Breath, and sometimes through the gentle orange/yellow still candle flame that accompanies me into the sweet embrace of the elements, of original being, of the heart of Fire, and into myself."

CHAPTER SIX

Righteous Rage

SPRING IS DARK, intense, and unafraid of her emotional intelligence, her "thinking heart." Strong, yet keenly sensitive, she is quick to react with a cannon shot of retributive wisdom to anything that smacks of unfairness, injustice, oppression, abuse, and degradation, particularly regarding women. Desperate for release, she comes to Fire for the express purpose of engaging in soul-work centering on the codependent ties binding her to an abusive relationship that has lasted six years.

To deepen the complex, we learn that she entered this love affair as a recovering alcoholic and drug addict with the best and bravest of intentions: a view to bright new beginnings and hope for renewed health and well-being. Her partner is a Native American named Coyote who, at the start, presented her with a persona that mirrored her own longing for abiding love grounded in respect and valuation.

Her actual experience with him however, culminates in a shattering of immense proportion. A collision between a single, iridescent raindrop and a shoulder of granite lodged against an unforgiving sky. Floating directionless, with sails unfurled, waiting for a strong trade wind, Spring loses her bearing. Becalmed, she is unable to move away from or toward anything that may hold hope for a brand new day.

During the process of preparing for the Fire ritual and in her stringent self-analysis, Spring correctly identifies her relationship with Coyote as one more rendition of her own addiction complex replete with all necessarily interconnected issues. Yet, she continues to expend ever-more precious emotional and psychophysical energy in fruitless attempts to repair the relationship. Efforts that describe a recurring cycle of departures, desperately tentative joyful returns, reconciliations leading to temporary appeasements, and again the resurgence of familiar disappointments leading to betrayal and departure. Gripped by a codependence that threatens to unhinge even her strongest self-defenses, Spring is trapped.

When I invite her to become involved in the Fire ritual, she has once again broken ties with Coyote, promising with the fervor of a thousand past promises that this time the severance will be final. Making a determined commitment to Fire and the ritual, Spring embarks on a pilgrimage, metaphorically speaking, to sacred places situated within the inner landscape of her own soul-referenced Self. In her journal writings these sacred places become temples of the goddesses Kali Ma, Ereshkigal, and Innana, the cave of her she-bear and then the blue and salty deeps of the dolphin playground. She describes the moth-devouring flame and celebrates the shimmering air in which butterflies uncannily reveal the gold hidden in their whispering wings. She applauds the fiery path of the eternally rising Phoenix, finally creating the "Possibilitree:" her own Tree of Life. This is the archetypal community, the gathering of spirits that congregate around and within Spring's abandonment and addiction complexes as she begins her therapeutic healing process with Fire in the heart of Nature.

In preparation for the ritual, she begins to retrace her steps to the beginning of her relationship with Coyote seeking a new understanding of the reality behind the recurring dynamic of idealized love devolving into lust and finally disappointment and grief. She hopes to be able to come to terms in this way with this relationship's disastrous consequences to her health and wellbeing. She also desperately needs to rediscover, to reclaim the Spring she once knew herself to be. She longs to move light-hearted toward a brightening new horizon, to rise and rise again like a moon-silvered ocean wave into a waiting and responsive world. And now she is resolved to cross this particular threshold with a fertile, nurturing, and power-filled Self in tow.

Gifting us with a profoundly poignant representation of her experience, Spring offers us a dazzling array of textual materials including twelve poems. Rich in symbolic and metaphoric imagery, her writings depict a six-year journey or, as she names it, her personal "tsunami" with Coyote. Collectively, her poems describe a circular, mandalic path divided into twelve self-contained segments.

Twelve is itself a power number dividing the human year and forming the astrological calendar replete with the life markers and destined pathways of the individual life. Twelve is also significant numerologically because of its calculational relationship to the numbers two, three, and four, already a thematic, archetypal pattern throughout this book.

Beyond being artistic expressions of her experience with Fire and the ritual, Spring's textual offerings also serve as formal witnesses to her soul tending. A process described by dislocation and relocation, confusion and clarification, catharsis and purification, and finally, release and liberation. Her journal and poems are an extraordinary testament to a woman's courage, radiance, creativity, strength, fragility, and willingness to undergo the most painful of transformations in her darkest hour.

I want to focus the discussion here on the righteous rage that transcribes itself most powerfully in Spring's journal. Like a lava flow in the blood, it burns, cleaves to, and infects her art. Her poems are riven landscapes littered with the emotional debris of her fractured Self.

Underscoring all of this is a life experience also shaped and informed by the wounded woman archetype that expresses itself in Spring's outrage against female oppression, and its consequent degradation and devaluation of women and their ways as witnessed throughout history. She righteously rages over the despoilment and loss of her love offering made to Coyote while at the same time suffering the culturally tempered chauvinism that is particular to some modern Native American men. She gives voice to all women and girls who, in a historically patriarchal world, have had their bodies, hearts, minds, and souls plundered, defiled, exploited, enslaved and burned.

Fire is a wake-up call. It is Earth's natural alarm system and the individual soul's. It is a formidable weapon. It is a warning cry and a reminder: we must recognize, name and say what we see. Nature teaches us the how-to, reminding us of the wisdom sources embedded in our natural, intuitive intelligence. Spring renders this for us with great passion and a terrible beauty.

Entry 1:

When I ponder the possibilities of this experience of engaging with Fire and of preparing for a Fire ritual, I know I want to document this process and the life experience I find myself in: the endings I'm engaged in right now. To explore the fault lines of faulty conclusions I've lived in—where they came from—to know the I that inherited cellular beliefs; the outcome that is/was my 58 years of life and the <u>new direction I seek</u>. That is, the accumulated experiences and new awareness born of returning and excavating myself from the depths of despair. I pray the Fire ritual opens the new beginnings inherent in endings and gives me guidance at the crossroads.

Entry 2:

Fire welcoming: Altar: Clear/clean area w/H20. Red cloth—1 white candle.

Willows placed in water. Smudge bowl w/home-grown white sage. Bell for Prayer-meditation—Burn sage—bring in directions—all my relations—spirit w/in & creator

Welcome the Fire and light candles—tears—big emotions—quieting self deeper, deeper—Fire is spirit-soul, soul lives in my heart—keep a flame lit in my heart-heart is altar for life. Center of gravity is w/in frame of reference—is w/in

*source of peace and power—attend to flame w/in on the altar
of my heart— ADD heart to altar—a purple amethyst heart.*

*Say a prayer for friendships past and for relationships just
ending. The present and future is built on the past, on death,
dying, passing, changing, letting go—flowing—remembering
lessons—compost for a richer future & present. The flame—is
a witness, observer, and recorder.*

*PUT picture of child-self under altar cloth. There is a bear
sleeping.*

The image of sleeping bear represents a powerful aspect of Spring's
Self both in terms of her need and in terms of her own transformative
experience with Fire. It is an experience that releases talents and skills
that conspire to move her toward *becoming* bear, a totemic presence
functioning in her soul.

Wilderness ranger and anthropologist David Rockwell discusses
the fact that among many Native American cultures, the hibernating bear is considered to be in an initiatory phase of its life cycle.
Following this thought metaphorically, within the safety of the bear
cave, one dies and is reborn seasonally. Also according to Rockwell,
the bear is considered a healing totem or spirit. Over generational
time many indigenous communities the world over observed the
plants that bears consumed and found that some of those same plants
had powerful and effective medicinal qualities. These plants became
the earliest sources of what we now call pharmaceutical medicine.

Spring's sleeping bear curls up in corners, or deep inside other
images, away from the storm raging on all fronts of the pages of her
journal. This aspect of her Self is in hibernation. Her she-bear is hiding, dreaming; she is unconscious yet processing; she is *gestating* in
her own potency; she is preparing, conditioning, and making ready
for an emergence. And so it is, that here in her own depths, where
the soul carries out the inner work of Self-transformation, in the bear
cave, the hollow of a tree, or an underground den, Spring undergoes
a soul initiation, a *rite de passage* of profound significance. It is an

experience that she is sometimes conscious of and in these lucid moments can see into the mysteries that will ultimately move her toward her own liberation, toward her own joy.

Many indigenous cultures mirror their own initiation rites such as vision quests on the hibernation season of the bear. Rockwell tells us that, "the isolation, the darkness of the hut or cave, the fasting and other elements of the bear [initiation] rites symbolized the candidate's ritual death." In this sense, during the preparation phase and during the Fire ritual itself, Spring undergoes a dying process where those aspects of her own wounded Self that no longer serve to enhance and protect her total well-being cease functioning. It is in the bear cave as sleeping bear that she dreams herself into becoming whom she needs to be in order to reemerge safely onto the surface of her life. But, until that moment of emergence, Spring positions herself firmly in her cave-stance, gathering to her Self all the necessary attributes she will need to cycle successfully into the next phase of healing as she moves toward wholeness of being.

Bears have also long been associated with Earth goddesses who both oversee the workings of Nature and *are* Nature themselves. Rockwell points to archeologist Marija Gimbutas' discussion of Eastern European Neolithic sites where hundreds of clay statuettes of bear headed women nursing cubs have been discovered. She calls them "bear nurses" describing them so beautifully as "epiphanies of the ancient Mother goddess in her animal form." Earth Mother in the image of sleeping bear comes to Spring's aid in the most immediate sense of things auguring an encounter connected to the Underworld.

Entry 3:

    Why ceremony? I am sacred—rituals, ceremonies affirm my sacredness. I honor myself & my connection to the Infinite. Ceremony affirms my sacredness. When I light the Fire altar— and deepen into my heart, belly, feelings, connection with the divine beyond separation—I return to my heartbeat—faithfully holding the drumbeat through it all—always here waiting for me to return to my soul or self.

Witnessing my melodrama: I've gone so far afield searching & have come home alive to my heartbeat drum. "I" must hold my broken heart, soothing, nurturing, balm of attention.

Playing the drum now is Inanna going deeper down the Spiral—deeper down into memories repressed, locked away from view: perceptions that nevertheless affect my life, surface up from the bottom of the ocean. Earthquakes send tsunami waves. Deep into the crevices of earthquake country to meet Ereshkigal, my repressed, unexpressed pain, sadness, anger, denial, betrayal.

My Sister-Self.

She has fangs. She has claws. Her hair is Fire; Her eyes blaze—She snarls & snaps, & growls & rants & raves, screams & hovers. She demands a voice. Kali Ma in all your blazing, terrible glory I behold you/me. I listen to your/my screaming anguish, your righteous snarling, your/my beautiful Rage. Lightning bolts fly, thunder roars, waves crash, earthquakes roll, winds howl, babies wail, women scream, children whimper, men battle and fall wounded. Grizzly bear roars a symphony of rage, despair, betrayal, loneliness, abandonment, hopeless, helpless, injustice, longing—exhaustion, anxiety, depression, aching, emptiness. I rage against the traffic, my friends, family, fighting with everyone—screaming in my car, crying to the dark night skies, the fucking distance of stars, the wound in Coyote's heart that keeps us apart, rage, rage, rage burning me up—

I witness it all as it rages around and thru me—long denied & in the writing and sharing—the healing begins.

So much of the pain caused by the denial, the looking away from, locked away in a closet, basement, sitting whimpering in a corner—the ignored child—"Why am I left, don't you want me? Aren't I enough? What's wrong with me?" I'm not enough—I shouldn't be—I don't deserve to live—I wish I hadn't lived! This is the Death Wish: the anchor that has held my ship down. That has kept me from sailing, going where the trade winds go—STUCK—anchored in a wish for death—not sailing on the flow of the goddess. Life—stagnating waters—

Ereshkigal & her sister Inanna—saw & cut, hack & chop together, sweating, laughing above they swing down with a mighty, mighty chop—All that rage energy is now channeled into getting free—directed at the cause for freedom, life. Mine is a flowing heart-self. Build my life, into my heart, into my belly. There is no longer a whirlwind ringing around inside in self-destructive hurricanes of confusion—delusion. Cutting the chords of destruction rather than cutting myself to pieces. Cut off from the flowing life—from my soul.

Peaceful waves lap against the sides of the boat, brilliant blue skies, forever horizons—rest—the boat slowly drifts on the trade wind flow—I surrender to

Her-Oneness. I am exhausted.

Candle flame—call the Fire, burn the sage. Ring the bell in the four directions— helpers—daffodils add to altar—trumpets heralding Spring's return. These are reflective—peaceful—quiet times. The ember is a surety of continuing. Resting before flaming up & enduring—deep in wisdom of lessons learned—the grey ashes surround me—a bed of experience—transforming—a cocoon. Sleeping —a bulb in the frozen soil—an ember in a bed of ashes—a caterpillar in a cocoon—a new Spring seeping up thru layers of earth—moments of sun on a stormy day.

Heartbeat drum—faithful—new crescent moon in a blinding black night. This tsunami has been 6 years long. It is built on the fault line of the San Andreas 58 years long."

Spring faithfully carries out her daily ritual with Fire at the altar she has prepared in her home. Like our Fire sister Kit, in connecting spiritually with the candle flame as her Spirit of Fire, she permits it to transport her into the kind of transpersonal state of mind necessary for her to access the depths of her own being. Here, she can collapse safely into her experience and, in the process, come to grips with what it asks of her, to follow where it is guiding her.

Spring collides with her Shadow almost immediately. She becomes enraged at her current situation: a broken heart, betrayed childhood, and a directionless life becalmed paradoxically in the centrifugal fury of the moment. But, in this headlong crash and because she has *intentionally* embarked on her encounter with Fire as a ritualized soul journey, she is careful to invoke the rare company of three most influential goddesses: the Sumerian Innana (later known as Ishtar in Mesopotamia) and her twin sister Ereshkigal, and Kali Ma from the Hindu Kush. She calls for them to rail and rage on with her, to hold her steady as she attacks, despairs, and disintegrates into her own crash and burn.

As Spring descends willingly into her own *nigredo,* her dark night, it is these three sacred ones who provide her with the array of resources necessary to safely reach bedrock in the soul. In fact, as we have already discussed, the journey toward illumination and encounter with the Divine often requires a confrontation with the darker aspects of the self; aspects that we keep secret in order to protect others; aspects that, once revealed and activated, make the whole enterprise of living a precarious one. In order to find her way into the Light, Spring must first sink into her rage, falling headlong into the dark embrace of her own abyss, where she begins to excavate long forgotten fragments of herself: fragments essential for healing and renewal. Innana and Ereshkigal will make sure that she lands firmly on both feet while Kali's Fire devotionals will light the way up and out when the time for Spring's return, her reemergence, arrives.

Let us now welcome Innana, and Ereshkigal onto these pages. According to artist and writer Rosanne Bane, Innana's sparkling crown is bejeweled with Heaven and Earth, with First Light of Dawn,

Moon, and the Evening Star. Like Artemis, her counterpart in ancient Greece, Innana is Lady of the Upperworld and sovereign over the wilderness and all creatures therein. Bane tells us that when Innana "stepped upon the clouds, lightning flashed and the rains fell, and where her footsteps touched the earth, plants sprouted and the animals quickened with new life."

Meanwhile, her twin, Ereshkigal, is the Lady of the Underworld and Keeper of the House of the Dead. As such, she holds dominion over all creatures' life and death cycles. In a strangely beautiful irony it is Ereshkigal who provides the gift of birth to creatures while Innana, under whose feet all living things grow, is personally barren.

With this twinned goddess, and with all sentient females, our procreative powers reside deep within our bodies where the uterine layers may be reached only by entering through the vulva, into the vaginal canal, journeying past the cervical gates, and then into the womb. This is a dim, watery world where a new life may begin or die in a single lunar cycle or be born into a sunlit world defined by a single solar star: our glorious, life-giving sun.

There are women who function as fully independent creatures, wielding our liberation like a rallying flag in times of distress. While, reluctantly or willingly, others become tethered to the bonds of responsible love to our mates, our children, families, friends, and communities. For some of us, who attempt to incorporate both into our lives, the inconsistencies may prove too great to bear. Consequently, we become split between these two imperatives becoming deeply contradicted in the process. For the lucky ones, at some point, this situation will force our attention, leading to an inner push for necessary change, resulting in a reintegration of the divided Self.

Let us remember that, like human beings, great divinities also strive for Self-discovery, to become soul-centered, and to become whole. They too undergo the process of individuation. Archetypes, gods and goddesses, and others who answer the call of a human soul for good company, support, and comfort while he or she is attempting to right things, often will take on the same task on their own terms, for their own good. Like Innana who also had to make a journey into the dark world of her twin sister Ereshkigal to save herself Spring must be willing to become an intimate of darkness, to know the shade as a lover and to brave the point of no return. There is no dream to be achieved, no life achievement or failure, no blessing or joy, and no stake to be claimed in the name of the Divine or the Dark Side that does not come with a price tag.

The archetypal pattern of the twinned deities is again weaving itself onto the pages of this book and into our field of consciousness. Innana's individuation process, the journey toward her own completion, provides a wonderful metaphor for the human dilemma, Spring's process and a soul map for those of us on the holy quest. It is worth the telling. Bear with me.

Innana, the Queen of Heaven, *listens in* to what is happening in the depths below heaven and Earth and hears her long-neglected sister Ereshkigal, Queen of the Underworld mourning the loss of her beloved consort, Gugalanna, the Bull of Heaven. As it is in the firmament below, so it is in the firmament above. The balance must be struck. Innana must make a journey that we all make one way or another. But this kind of pilgrimage to a different darker sacred place requires her to be stripped of all external finery—signs and signifiers from the upper world have no place in the soul's dark night. At each step of the way, moving deeper into the Underworld and closer to her sister she is stopped unable to proceed until she has gifted the Gate Keepers her most precious valuables. Even more significantly, when she asks why she is required to pay her way forward as it were, the reply is, "but that is just the way of the Underworld."

In order to go deeper, Innana is compelled to hand over precisely the objects that testify to her queenly stature and power as a goddess: her bejeweled queen's cane, her turban and royal gown, her golden ring, lapis lazuli necklace, and her sacred prayer beads. Even more significant is the demand for her surrender to the fact that there is no necessary rhyme or reason to anything when one undertakes a journey through the Underworld—into one's own depths. Having given away all tokens of the powers and attributes that make up who she is, defenseless, and naked, a vulnerable Innana arrives to face her despairingly lonely, envious twin sister neglected by her beloved twin over the ages and now enraged and vengeful. In this precarious state, one bitter glance from Ereshkigal "says it all." Innana is slain, her body hung out to rot. Please believe me: we each have our own Ereshkigal secreted away in the darkest chambers of our soul who desperately needs tending to, who needs to be loved, and above all who needs Light.

Here we are reminded again that the descent into the abyss can be life threatening. Schizophrenia is the testament. It is a world representing the greatest fear of the inspired seeker of soul: stepping past the point of no return. To venture past this point is to enter alone into the pathological dimensions of the metaphysical world. This is a world where an uninformed, unbridled imagination is caught helplessly in the grip of a powerful complex or system of complexes that draw into their gravitational pull "others" who attach themselves to the heart, mind and soul with the force of a stranglehold: a permanent possession.

Veronica Goodchild cautions that "falling into the shadows threatens our very life and identity, and the descent puts us in the wilderness, in the Underworld, where we slowly dissolve and decay, where we betray the self we thought we were so attached to, where all our identifications are dislodged." Fortunately, Spring knows that there is a particular art to this kind of thing. Her carefully transcribed journey into the depths of her own righteous rage is careful and precise with a constant noting of the exit signs. She is safely contained within the formal parameters of the preparation rites and the psychodynamic presence of Fire in her preparation process, her journal, and her poems.

The great goddess Innana too is not alone. Remember, when one sets out intentionally on the search for Self, for meaning, and for encounter with the Divine, one should be accompanied right from the start by boon companions. As discussed earlier, these may be literal companions: true friends, a therapist, teachers, close family, your spiritual circle or the metaphysical influence of benevolent transcendent symbols, visions, revealed insights, sudden illuminations, dream figures, and spirit beings.

So it is with Innana, where, through clever tricks and even smarter tomfoolery, her devoted personal priestess Ninshubur and two tiny, androgynous creatures, Gala-tura and Kur-jara, find the way to appease Ereshkigal. Although still insisting upon the righteous reasons for her pent up rage against her neglectful twin, Ereshkigal is nevertheless beside herself with grief. Innana's companions succeed by lovingly and generously responding to Ereshkigal's sincere regret at what has happened to her sister, her own source of the Light she so desperately yearns for. They try all means to convince the goddess of the Land of the Dead to release her sister and permit her to return to Heaven and Earth above. Ereshkigal finally agrees but only with the promise that Innana's beloved husband Dumuzi reside in the Underworld with her for half the year providing precious love and Light. Innana agrees and balance and harmony grounded in illuminated love have been restored.

When the defenses of the Underworld—our own dark abyss have been breached, an annual tribute on pain of death or wholesale destruction is set in stone. This tribute can be thought of as a kind of soul tax that holds an individual existence, whether human or divine, for ransom. Innana had to give up everything to get to her own twinned self to heal and resolve what had become a death-dealing inner construct threatening to tip the balance of creation itself! This is also the classic Demeter and Persephone or Isis and Osiris myth replayed in ancient Sumeria by Innana, Ereshkigal and Dumuzi. It is a mythological rendering of the creation process, of sustaining life in its cyclic aspect, its seasonal imperative. It is also a reflective metaphor for the human soul's ritual circumambulatory search for its own origin myth, meaning, and purpose. Jung reminds us that the process of individuation is a lifetime endeavor that it is, at the deepest levels, a spiritual imperative. If what you want it is a self-help recipe, with ten easy steps, five simple promises, and total healing from a weekend intensive, please don't attempt it.

And so we see Spring pushed down into a spiral of depression, sorrow, and alienation. Now she becomes frightened of what she has bravely released from her own private Pandora's Box. But, the triadic power of Kali, Innana, and Ereshkigal holds her firmly in its grasp. The goddesses appear in a glorious display of symbol, image, and mythopoetics. We feel them at work in the storm of words heaving and pounding on the pages of her journal. We see them dancing, and spinning out healing insights, teachings, and guidance for her to follow. We hear both their sweet and fearful siren voices in the poetry that bears the seeds of her renewal and rebirth.

In fact, Spring's journal *is* her safe haven, and a silent witness, as alive and vibrant as any other. It becomes the bear cave; her witch's cauldron; her surgical knife; her own secret alchemical chamber. When she fearfully backs away from the process, when she begins to constrict and collapse under the weight of it all, she turns to her Fire altar in her home, the candle flame, and her journal. And, with her experience being so deeply connected to the creative process, it is imperative that she not retreat from the increasing intensity. Her journal keeps her on track. In fact, it is her way of maintaining order in the midst of chaos. In one moment, it is the sorcerer's den where the predicament of her wounding calls forth an alchemy urging transformation. In the next, it is a cauldron fired by the flames of her rage and an urging to stew up a strange and healing brew.

Veronica Goodchild tells us, "depression or melancholy, far from being a symptom to be cured, is the call that first attempts to restore us to a state, not of archaic identity, but eventually to a differentiated consciousness that does not separate above from below, and in which the mystery of life can once again be embraced and lived on a renewed level."

Spring's journal entries and poetry reflect this harmonizing process. She usually begins, ends, or punctuates the middle of an entry by describing a ritual act, or providing salutary remarks that describe her awareness of her own spiritual center, her truth, her sense of the Divine within her, and her irrepressible optimism. These expressions form a structure of words on which she can fasten the pain and sorrow, the dislocation, and the disintegration, until finally, like the Phoenix rising from the ashes, awkwardly at first, then exquisite in flight, she is free.

༄༄༄

As we continue to move through Spring's writings, we see the appearance of two new powerful symbols of transformation. First, we hear of "a bulb in the frozen soil" gathering up the heat that comes from bearing within itself life giving and life sustaining nutrients. This is a potentiality that, while being held captive in the frozen bind of a world grown still for winter, remains wakeful for the moment when a whisper of sunlight will trigger a burst of life and a rush to emerge resplendent. Second, she applauds "a caterpillar in a cocoon," one of the most powerful metamorphic processes in Nature.

Butterflies and moths abound as both symbol and metaphor in Spring's poetry during her preparation process and work with Fire. While her experience is manifestly echoed in the chronicle of the caterpillar creating its own shining chrysalis as it moves inexorably toward its own becoming. Then, as a fully-fledged butterfly glimmering in the translucent air, pursuing a moment of exquisite bliss, it rests on a tender petal, fiercely making love with another fragile beauty, and then disappearing as softly as it had entered into our frame of reference.

Now Spring finds herself compelled to continuously circle back to revisit old wounds newly reopened or as yet unattended. These turnings and re-turnings are a spiraling, dynamic constant in the process of individuation. The transforming Self demands it.

Entry 4:
    I return—turn back and face the ghosts that shadow my
    every step. The shaming sadness—my broken heart in her arms

trailing of tears, of blood trailing thru centuries of lifetimes—of women's lives, of being bought & sold, punished for being bold. Enslaved & chained, learned helplessness, learned hope-lessness, victim, burned and battered, controlled, owned. The ghost of righteous rage—caged & forbidden—turned against myself, my sisters—righteous rage flies from my lips burning through the walls, bars, harems, whorehouses, housewives, no names of our own. The ghost of illusion, of love—Love cost me myself. I must earn love. Sex is love. Am I loveable? What do I do to make you love me?

The steel door over my heart—I play it like a drum—sing-ing, soothing, building trust in my self slowly ... a relationship with my SELF of dependability, stability, healing, nurturing—ghosts are here for healing. I face them. I embrace them/me/child-self. Slowly, soothing, building trust.

We need to explore Spring's "ghosts of righteous rage," and the "ghosts of illusion" more deeply because her ghosts do haunt her dreadfully. In fact, we all endure our own hauntings.

In many cultural traditions some ghosts are conceived as spirits who do not perceive themselves as fully alive or fully dead. Their tor-ment consists in being unable to understand let alone appreciate the dimension of existence in which they find themselves. They experi-ence themselves as empty and, consequently yearn for and strive to break through into this dimension, wreaking havoc in the lives they choose to vicariously live through.

Then, there are "hungry" ghosts who function from a confusion of remembered rage and desire and are tormented by unfulfilled crav-ings. Once they are able to elicit recognition from and access to sus-ceptible humans, they prove to be insatiable in their demands for immediate gratification. They are spirits who cannot let go of their previous existence as humans and consequently remain frighteningly attached to the living.

There are those among us who are sensitive to the presence of ghosts or spirits of the dead and yet remain unafraid. Like Jung, in his paranormal encounters with the dead, we form relationships with, carry out tasks for, and negotiate a truce with those ghosts that enter into our purview. We do this through praying, chanting, ritual purifications, food offerings, channeling, and sometimes, simple conversation to discover their own specific needs so we can address them positively and constructively to their benefit and to ours.

Afflicted beings irresistibly drawn to a particular individual like iron to a magnet, ghosts may also appear as self-afflictions. They may be our own ancestors whose personal fates and unrealized dreams are reborn into this life via our DNA. Their destinies, reaching to the beginning of time and carved into our bone and blood, spill out once again only to be redrawn onto the canvases of our own lives.

Spring's ghosts reside and function in all her works. They also haunt us by extension. They are not only related to the collective, historical experience of women, but also to her/my personal history of sexual exploitation in childhood and the burn of the sin that coils like a shamed serpent in the cicatrice of one's own secret ecstasies.

For Spring, and all women who have been injured in this way, our ghosts are important because their insistent presence reveals a very real need on our/their part to be permitted to speak through us for the sake of justice, truth and peace. Spring allows them this privilege. I am reminded of Jung's experience of being haunted by several ghosts who arrive at his house and, via several paranormal experiences, manage to pique his curiosity, thereby getting his attention. When he inquires as to the reason for their presence, they answer, "We have come back from Jerusalem where we found not what we sought."

Jung's ensuing communications with them result in *The 7 Sermons of the Dead*, written or channeled over three evenings at their request. "As soon as I took up the pen," he tells us, "they vanished, the room quieted, the haunting was over."

In fact, Jung spent a great deal of time working with stone at the Tower of Bollingen, his home and personal retreat. This is the shamanic Jung, in his archaic nature. While working on a number of stone tablets on which he lists his ancestors, "I became aware of the fateful links between me and my ancestors," he confesses, going on to say that there is an "impersonal karma within a family that is passed on from parents to children and so on," and how he feels with certainty that he has "to complete, or perhaps continue, things which previous ages had left unfinished." This is important to consider as we give Spring's ghosts their due respect.

Spring's words run the gauntlet across the pages of her journal, and in her poems we hear a chorus of women's cries, gnashing teeth, and the death cry of a child's innocence irrevocably corrupted, forever lost. Her words rip and shred, the tears sting, the person she thinks her Self to be is torn apart. Nevertheless, it must be named, it must be said, and it must be done.

Feminist scholar Catherine Keller insists that, "there can be no doubt that woman has been trapped, trivialized, and exploited in these margins of heaven and earth. Woman projected as Madonna mediates between the divine and the human; as Whore she seduces the human toward the animal. Woman has been rendered multilaterally marginal."

And Spring is fiercely breaking through her own marginalization. She is struggling to get herself and her ghosts back onto the center of the page until they, like Jung's insistent specters, are finally appeased. "Inner peace and contentment," Jung tells us, "depend in large measure upon whether or not the historical family which is inherent in the individual can be harmonized with the ephemeral conditions of the present."

Another of Spring's stabilizing archetypes is named Drumming Woman in her journal. Spring holds onto her hand drum as a drowning woman would to a lifeline. On the one hand, she plays it gently, rhythmically, and steadily like the second hand on an antique wristwatch or a heartbeat safely in love. On the other hand, she rolls out a beat like thunder, crashing with the voice of an avenging angel. Then again, her drum also serves as a constant companion to her daily meditations as she prepares for the Fire rites.

Spring's drum as literal object and as metaphor for the heartbeat of Earth Mother centers and enlivens her like the planet's own steady beating heart secures all her children. Seconds before spinning out of control she begins to drum and is drawn back to the here and now. The drum tempers her rage, and maintains her sanity. Her drum *is* Spring's taut and swollen heart.

Goddesses and their devotees have danced to the drum throughout the ages. In its archetypal significance as herald, the drum also calls in Spring's helping spirits, those already identified and others who may appear unbidden. Pinkola-Estes agrees, telling us, "The skin or body of a drum determines who and what will be called into being."

The drum also inspires in Spring the martial qualities essential to safe inner journeying. These qualities secure the return from the start: intentionality and intelligence, commitment and courage, focus, direction, and persistence.

Even more significantly, in this case, a drum at war is used to provide coded messages to warriors in the field. It keeps the fight strong and the warriors brave hearted. It also maintains discipline and, when necessary, can beat out a victory march that resounds through the air like bolted lightning. Let's not forget that Spring is in the battlefield, fighting at every level of her being for her Self. Her small hand drum is needed for all it represents.

Entry 5:

What is this repeating pattern? Men who are weak, lost, selfish, no love to show—my biological father, not available, undependable, doesn't show up emotionally or even physically, betraying—other women, cheating, lying—my mother's pattern learned. Men's privilege is to act this way, and women have no choice but to tolerate it? There are more questions than answers today.

The stepfather next—calculating, manipulating, evil, wicked, cheating, lying predator, damaged, stuck, driven. Desperate mother, 2 small children pay the price for her lack of self-respect, her lack of choices, her lack of support, recognition, skills—voice—generations of women w/o voices, choices. Learned behavior, generations of men—emotions blocked, hearts w/steel doors, locked—sex & anger only feelings allowed you. This is the enemy—this is a man who wants to prey on your own children, family, lovers, and wives.

I tried marriage to a man—heart locked away behind steel doors. Sex & anger—only emotions shown—thinkin' I could love him well—sex is love, how can I earn your love, how can I ever be a Playmate Bunny? You and I challenged the first few layers of those patterns—refusing to have a piece of paper (marriage license)—be a definition of who we were. But I challenged the deeper fault lines—your privileges of maleness, your emotional absence, your lack of accountability, your cheating, lying, and flirting, your unavailability—challenged your notion of yourself. You enjoy the privileges maleness gives you—your laziness & selfishness & fear—& you lost me. And now I get to the bone-Skeleton Woman, curled up foetus and Vulture Sister—that sister is on this bloody corpse—road kill—I need the tainted flesh gone—I need it all off! Give me back my bones! Let me start over—Free! Free! Free! "My emancipation doesn't fit in your equation." Lauryn Hill.

Spring's she-bear steps forth here. Turning into a wild woman she tumbles into the arms of her own untamed self. At some times, she surrenders appropriately to an overriding need to disintegrate. At others, in order to pull herself together, she is sometimes called to tear others apart but carefully and with insight. Again, gifts and qualities that Innana, Ereshkigal, and Kali Ma share and demand of their devotees.

But now a turning point: two new and highly evocative archetypal presences make themselves known: Skeleton Woman and Vulture Sister = emancipation. Spring must become Vulture Sister to pick and peel the flesh rotting off the bones of her shattered yet still lovely skeletal being.

This is a formidable ruthless image that mirrors an aspect of Spring's wounded self in it's most pure and indestructible sense: a form waiting to be purified at the level of bone, a form requiring all newly revealed surface fractures to be soldered by flame. Skeleton Woman is compelled to surrender to her Vulture sister, to the caustic burn of the rapid-fire pull of her razor-sharp beak. Here a shocking self-consumption takes place that necessarily leads to the metamorphosis critical to achieving an illuminated higher Self at peace within.

As our tri-goddess constellation insists, cultivation of beauty in the midst of dire necessity is critical. And so Spring is obliged, bone-on-bone, to polish Skeleton Woman to a pearlescent sheen that will outshine even the Moon at her loveliest.

There is surrender and sacrifice required here. And there is much unbearable pain! Spring gives herself over to Vulture Sister's carri-on ways. Have you ever picked on yourself with vindictive brutality again, and again, and again until the pain eases up, the guilt fades away, and the sting of shame finally recedes? Yes. But, here is the gift. It is only when Skeleton Woman is purified and prepared, that Spring can flesh her out anew, wrap her in expertly treated and tanned virgin skin, and brighten her with jewel eyes that see everything in a new light. Jungian psychologist and feminist writer Clarissa Pinkola-Estes insists: "This is our meditation practice as women, calling back the dead and dismembered aspects of ourselves, calling back the dead and dismembered aspects of life itself. The one who re-creates from that which has died is always a double-sided archetype. The creation Mother is also the Death Mother and vice versa. Our work is to ap-prehend the timing of both; to allow what must die to die, and what must live to live."

Spring's wounds still live, the scars painful to the touch. Fire brands of shame glow inside her body, rifle through her mind, and shoot right through to her soul. Her righteous rage at the history of patriarchal genocide directed at women's ways scorches the pages of her journal and hounds her poems. Her words are like flames gone wild, they leap over space and time testifying to church legislated burnings of women practicing folk medicine, and to the biblically approved rape of women and girls as bona fide spoils of war.

This is the process of dismemberment: the dissecting of a soul ever searching for the mediating Light of the Divine. At one moment Spring unravels on the page and in her lived life and in the next she is in the process of reintegration. She can do this because she is held safely within the parameters of the Fire rites and by her Fire sisters whose act of witnessing itself is a psychodynamic containing space for a soul deeply engaged in its own tending.

When Spring describes a "broken heart in her arms trailing of tears, of blood trailing thru centuries of lifetimes of women's lives," she is referring not only to the copious amounts of ordinary tears shed. The mythopoetic language of her journal entries and poems forms a rushing undercurrent of energy, drenching the evocative and sacred images that inhabit her writings with a river of tears.

Tears are necessary to initiate, sustain, and then seal the disintegrative process, becoming in turn creative, uniting, healing, and restorative agents of change. It is in these kinds of tears that we find the healing long searched for, and transformative insights gratefully embraced. In this way, we make our own medicine and begin to nurture, nourish, and re-create those aspects of our selves needing just that.

Spring's experience participating in the Fire ritual is powerful and resonates for some time afterwards.

Entry 6:
 During the Fire ceremony I invoked the goddess Kali—to dismantle aggression, suppression, depression, repression & she walked with me for weeks after as I raged & named the

enemy of life—named the ghosts, named the lurking Beast, & then I claimed my voice, my passion, my power to alter my own best interests—NO LONGER ... instead shine the light of illumination into these caves into my deeper cellular memories. Release, release, release, burn and burn—illuminate—transform. The flames become violet, purple, fuchsia, blue power, voice wails. Maleness Yang-God—Pink-red, nurturing, devotional feminine Ying-goddess—protective, and soothing. Together violet -flame invited into cellular changes, memories burn, and transform. Golden goddess fill all the voids of transformation w/abundance & once again a golden ember in a bed of ashes of yesterdays—contained, self warming—self restoring content to be, to radiate Golden goddess of Hope.

Entry 7:

DRIFTWOOD ON MY ALTAR

Emotions float to the surface of my mind. Twisted pieces of driftwood scars, deep gashes. Who knows where they come from, or what they have been thru. Drifting into my awareness, seeking to be discovered, witness, translated, recognized, deciphered, embraced, healed.

Great, overwhelming, sorrowful emotions rush into my awareness each time my life slows down, I keep myself busy ... running ... away from these feelings?

Perhaps I'll take the time, this slowed down time, to sit and listen ... watch the memories drift like bubbles to the surface of my awareness. Perhaps, I'll look and listen. I did make a promise to myself to listen, pay attention, and heal my inner landscape. So maybe this is the time, the opportunity to descend into the cauldron deep, dark, nebulous, foreboding. Walk the spiral staircase downward into my deepest gut, where I have shoved memories too painful to grasp. Hidden & ignored, they ferment & they claw their way to the surface *against my every will. I will descend. I will seek Ereshkigal my twin Sister Self who embodies the pain, whose body holds the rememberings, scarred and gashed, she can't, won't, forget. She holds the memories I have been too afraid to face.*

I will embrace these hurt places and let love bathe the wounds. I know half the wound is caused by being ignored. This I know and must not do to myself ... what others have done ... learned behavior... I will care for, pay attention to these emotional memories, trusting I will keep my word to myself. NOW pay attention, translate, decipher, embrace and heal.

Emotions ... the sign posts, arrows, pointing the way, directing me to these places of pain, hurt, rejection, regret, abandonment, betrayal, sorrow, loneliness, confusion. Naming them, recognizing them, brings tears and relief. I know their names; they are not complete strangers. We have met before; they eagerly await my presence, witnessing these crimes against myself, witnessing and applying the soothing balm of recognition and grief that these crimes happened to the young child that was/is me. Vowing to protect her/me now. Vowing I am valuable and precious and worth loving and protecting.

My gut relaxes ... roar of turbulent, crashing surf ... oceans of pain ... subside into lapping waves, soothing, calming. The driftwood takes on the shapes of healing spirals, Mother goddesses I carry home and put on my altar.

Here Spring is beginning to understand that anger and love are not necessarily opposed. Rather, her righteous rage has a connecting function to her own inner depths where the work is being done while, at the same time, a healing and conciliatory effect is taking place. Justified anger is often the necessary, initiatory move toward acknowledging that something is terribly wrong somewhere. Christian feminist Beverly Wildhung-Harrison so eloquently states, "anger is always a vivid form of caring."

Ironically, when one is able to show genuine caring and concern even through perspectives informed by anger, situations may be resolved in highly effective ways. "All serious human moral activity, especially action for social [or individual] change," Wildhung-Harrison says, "takes its bearings from the rising power of human anger. Such anger is a signal that change is called for, that transformation in relations is required."

Absent feelings are not as close to love as anger is. When we confront another or ourselves in anger we are in essence forcing attention upon very real needs. We are demanding to be heard, to be valued, and to be loved with a corresponding emotional response that serves as a diffuser or as a peacemaker. At the same time, we are also dealing with a profoundly volatile and destructive emotion. So, for the sake of balance, we need to love our anger back into its rightful place in the wider economy of the soul.

The Vietnamese Buddhist teacher Thich Nhat Hanh tells us that the key to dealing with our anger is to use a state of consciousness referred to as mindfulness in which we are able to realize that anger is a part of our own selves. Anger belongs to us. It has its nature, its uses, and its purposes. Our responsibility is to tend to our anger so that it does not spiral out of control ceasing to be of service to us. Being mindful of our anger, we choose instead to recognize and embrace it while at the same time becoming acutely aware of what is going on in the present moment. We accept it and permit it to be present *on our own terms*. In this way, we can consider alternative ways to deal with whatever is confronting us. Learning to use anger as a positive, constructive energy, while keeping a disciplined rein on it, is an act of love toward one's Self.

Meanwhile, Spring is rooting her way through the inner process that she describes as an excavation. She pries open hidden wounds carefully examining scars recently healed. She digs deeper and deeper into the far reaches of her childhood. She relives the solitary suffering and the shame, the dislocations, and a lifetime of soul-crushing disappointment.

But this time, placing it all in the world of a ritually defined encounter with Fire, Spring finally brings love into the equation. In this section of her journal, at the beach with the driftwood and the waves, she begins the process of loving herself into wholeness. It has been a courageous move on her part to let her rage run the gamut. Wildhung-Harrison applauds this kind of move. "We should not make light of our power to rage against the dying of the light," she says, "it is the root of the power of love."

Entry 8:
 Memories of the Fire ceremony return. The place—on the Earth. The reaching trees, the rise and fall of wind, the answering, responding bird calls, clouds over sun, sun shining through clouds
 All participants in the ceremony to be seen, heard, felt by the listening, learning, attentive heart.
 The memories of the ceremony are as much the place, the Fire, sky & water & animals—spirits, guides, ancestors as the human beings, the Fire sisters present.
 Then, the dolphins came in when we called for messages and guidance for me.
 Dolphins came gaily, frolicking, playful in—they said, "You've cried an ocean—now come in and swim w/us." My heart leapt w/joy, fullness, playfulness, strength, family, and adventure—did I say connection—family ♥ joyful—Blessed Be.
 My reluctant, sore heart hesitates. So much joy? I notice the pause—I respect the hesitation feelings—afraid to risk feeling again—happiness—last time my happiness depended on someone outside myself—my balance was outside—this time the happiness is w/in me. In the Fire ceremony there was no disappointment lurking around the corner. No lies or pretense to uncover. No calculating to discover. Just simple, childlike, pure, innocent joy & fun, pleasure, flowing from

life herself—from the sisters present —sharing, openhearted, brave sisters—I love circles of sisters. Breaking through the tsunami. Dolphins swim through this tsunami & catch the waves of pleasure—

Dolphins Dance Beyond—
Beyond the labyrinth—Beyond the reign of pain into Recovery, Rebirth,
Re-member-ing, I am my Beloved—I am Presence—I am a spark of Infinite Fire
I am moving on

During this Fire ceremony there has been much dying—releasing, letting go—making room for the new Fire of life—making room began with recognizing—<u>descending</u> into my own depths—embracing the wounds, releasing the stories. Even tho' I am still <u>recognizing</u> and <u>releasing</u>—I know the lesson—Recognize, Release—Reason Revealed & soon I will claim my new Self ♥

It's tricky—dealing with & healing from obsession, addiction. In the beginning of this Fire ceremony process, I dedicated my ceremony to explore this six-year emotional tsunami—that took me to the depths for years & the heights only for moments. Now it's all expressed, released—a wail on the wind—fists pounded on the ground—chopped thru the death wish anchor, yet I must return a few more times to leave flowers on the graves. It's been a bittersweet love affair with suffering. Suffering feels like a fur coat I clutch around me thinking this is all there is for me. Thinking this is comfort.

So glad and blessed for this opportunity to PROCESS until I'm done. Having a place to express all I've experienced. I've grown & having a silent witness to read this is part of the process as well. Thank you for this opportunity to heal. Ismana, your presence, essence. My midwife thru this birthing

. . . blessed be. Feeling guided, clear, hopeful—Spring.

If you will recall, I was guided to place a beautiful bronze Shiva Nataraj on the Eastern altar in the arbor at Indian Canyon. The Nataraj is Shiva dancing creation into being: universes, galaxies, solar systems, constellations, and all things bright and beautiful.

During the Fire ritual itself, Spring invokes Shiva's Shakti in her form as the goddess Kali Ma, the Black Mother. Standing close to Fire, in the arbor at Indian Canyon, she sings down Kali with such power that flames roar in response, leaping eagerly toward her, causing her Fire sisters pangs of fear. But she stays resolute, moving closer to the Fire singing ever more fervently.

The world surrounding joins in. The wind rises, letting loose a shower of leaves that carpet the ground in filigreed patterns of gilded sunlight. Cicadas join in, a thousand voices strong, hawks pierce the air with their cries and, just for a moment or two, the ever-raucous blue jays and ravens are silenced. Artemis' beloved twin, the sun god Phoebus-Apollo shines directly onto the bronze statue of Shiva Nataraj spinning it into gold.

According to Veronica Goodchild, it is important for us to understand that Shakti is "a manifestation of Spirit that mobilizes a woman's imperfections and limitations until they become allies and helpers – a salve for the perfectionists among us! She is the energy of Shiva who, without her, would be a corpse."

This is how things are for Spring! She has moved closer toward the release, liberation, and reclamation of her Self and her life as it moves beyond the emotional entrapment of her abandonment and wounded feminine complexes. Her archetypal cluster now includes dolphins that swim joyously in her vision in the arbor, and she has gone to the ocean's edge, taking with her a heart still sparking firebrands in search of a conflagration but tempered by a newly composed and more deeply informed Self.

Pinkola-Estes quotes Jung, who says, "When spirit becomes heavy, it turns to water. Therefore the way of the soul leads to the water."

Spring's joyous dolphins hold within them the magical mystery of the paradoxical union of Fire and water. Like sparks of fiery energy, they leap and play in the icy blue depths of a salt water world, speeding mercurial through waves dappled in cerulean and lapis hues, displaying a rapture of loving. They mirror Spring's longing to learn again how to live a passionate, liberated, loving life in a gently playful way that will not drown out her righteous rage for life, truth, and justice. The dolphins will show her the way.

They will midwife her newly born Self carefully and beautifully, teaching her about communality, self sacrifice, nonjudgmental loving, and, above all, generosity of spirit. Through their healing ministrations, she will realize that more than serving her Self and her own needs, serving others and providing for their needs is where she will ultimately find the kind of inspired love she yearns for: a divine Grace that falls like spring rain on parched ground.

Twelve poems follow as Spring's parting gift.

Romance

Romance, a Knight on a Horse
Indian Brave Bareback
Tipi on the plains
Whisk me away—somehow someway
Against all the odds
Love is enough
Love will find a way
Illusions, Delusions

Tending the Flame

Tend the flame faithfully
Burning on the altar of my heart
In ember-subdued
Hidden in the grey ash of what was
I am that one tiny ember shrouded in grey ash
Surviving the fiery destruction of what was
The aching, the breaking, the burning
When your heart breaks & breaks & breaks
Then what?

Barely breathing

My heart wants to stop
To freeze time
Resisting the reality of separation.

I'm at a standstill
Barely breathing
Shocked silence

Labyrinth

Circling around
The labyrinth of your lies
Looking for the basis
Of your betrayals

Sinking into the confusion
Of your cruelty

Despairing in the depth
Of your deceit

Collapsing in the coldness
Of your cruelty

Serpentine labyrinth
Of my own demise
Disguised as devotion

Circling around
Confused, collapsing, sinking, dizzy
My own demons draw closer
Unwanted, abandoned, betrayed, used
Ignored, unseen, damaged, devalued
My earliest experiences
Traced the trail
Of the labyrinth
I now traverse

A path set in stone
Shape-shifting demons
Become children forlorn
Whimpering in corners

Abandoned for so long
Hungry, tearful eyes
Breakthrough the dark
My heart awakens
And sends forth sparks
Of healing recognition
She's no longer forsaken

Embraced, retrace the labyrinth
With angelic Grace
Safe, sacred, sincere
Within there is this place

I can no longer dwell here

I can no longer dwell in this place
A sinking quicksand of sadness
Drowning in despair

I can no longer linger
In this crying place
Spirit wings broken
Struck down
By your cold cruelty

I must not linger here
Looking back at the desolation
That has become my life
My heart becomes a tombstone

I must not linger here at a standstill
Becoming a pillar of salt
My tears crystallizing
Around me
Entombing me
In this deadly despair

Secret doorway

"Discontent is the secret doorway to
significant and life-giving change"

Each insult and injury
Created a hairline crack in my heart
Until a chasm of discontent
An arroyo of sorrow
A gorge of hurt
A canyon of cruelty
An abyss of dissatisfaction
A roaring ravine of neglect
Deepened within me

I stood on the volcano's edge
The crest of the wave
The tip of the arrow
Flying across the abyss

A secret doorway opened
A rainbow bridge appeared
A life change is happening
Discontent has disappeared

Moth to a flame

I am moth to flame
Participating in my own destruction
Each time I come to you

You are a feeble flame
Offering no warmth
Flaring up only briefly
As you consume me

The butterflies did not return this year

The butterflies did not return this year
Scorching indifference burned their fragile wings
Calculating cruelty crushed their spirits

Treacherous deception drowned them in despair
Selfish manipulation sexploited their beings
Lack of appreciation proves you cannot care
Your heart is rigid and arctic and drove them away

Until only
A fantasy of butterflies
A faint whisper of wings
A wisp of sublime colors
Remain

Flaming butterfly

I am no longer a moth to flame
But a flaming butterfly
Rising from the ashes
Of my own destruction
Savoring all life, sweet nectar
After nearly starving
On your cold cruelties
Your bitter fruit

Your web of deception
Held me for so long
Woven by the sad, broken
Part of myself
Believing cruel betrayal
Was deserved

Your web was so convincing
You believe your own lies
You believe you're kind
But you are cruel
You believe you're a victim
But you are a predator
You believe you are giving
But you're a thief
You believe you are free
But you're locked in the cage of your past, your fears
You believe you're a friend
But you're an enemy

In the light of my flaming wings
I see the truth
I see the illusion of what

I thought you were
Who I wished you were
Who you promised to be
A friend, a partner
Honest, sharing, caring

Phoenix Arise

My spirit calls me from the graveyard of my dreams

Rise up fiery Phoenix
Of every woman's soul
Broken by a man so cold
Been bought and sold
Manipulated and controlled
Raped and owned
Silenced and chained
Told she has no brains
Ignored and denied
Sterilized and burned

Tables about to turn
The goddess returns
This is the best part
She rises in my heart
My will to thrive is stronger
Than your weak cruelty
My dreams a grave no longer

I want a partner

My needs are good and right
I want a partner
Tonight it's just not you

I'm a rose in full bloom
A garden of possibilities
I look forward to sharing
All that can be
Good intentions, clear sight
Loving kindness, spirit bright
Passionately soft kisses
And juicy delights

Shared silence, where no secrets dwell
One look of compassion, nothing to tell
Space alone, some to share
Sacred presence, natural to care

This is what I give and am ready to receive
Please tell no lies, I want so to believe
No disappointment round every corner
No lies to uncover
No rages to fear
No omissions to discover
No secrets hiding here

I plant these seeds of possibility
Knowing they will bloom into
A POSSIBILITREE
Blessed be

I am

I am
Defending myself
Distancing myself
Deciding myself
Directing myself
Discovering myself
Determining myself
Designing myself
Delighting in myself
Dreaming myself

I am
Seeking myself
Supporting myself
Surprised by myself
Satisfied by myself

I am recognizing myself
Reasoning with myself
Releasing myself
Realizing myself
Receiving myself
Reverencing myself

Bright Eyed Woman of the Highlands

I stand on the brink of my reality
A bright-eyed woman of the highlands
Beckons from beyond.
Her presence births seedlings
Of possibilitrees in my heart

A startling radiant dawn
Fractures my midnight
Long submerged
Forgotten radiance awakens
Reaching, remembering, regaining
What once was and shall be

She calls me
She is me
She invites me into a garden of fertile soils
With enchanted seeds
Of possibilitrees

Self-care, self-knowledge, the seedlings
An expanding, expressive, exciting life
The sweet fruit
Liquid love pours forth from Creator
Nurturing this promise
Of a new garden

A woman remembering her sacred self
Excavating herself from lifetimes of enforced forgetting
No time to look back take back
Only moving forward
As a consecrated midwife of my own birth
As a roaring dancer,

A soaring eagle dancer,
A dreaming dolphin dancing
With Creator's drumbeat in my heart

—We've got to get ourselves back to the garden.

CHAPTER SEVEN

The Visitor

IN THE ARBOR at Indian Canyon, the blue-tipped flames are waist high, burning orange, gold, and red, fanned gently by a warmly scented spring breeze defying the darkening, storm-filled sky. I stand at the edge of the fire pit, as close to the flames as possible and begin to carry out my personal work. In this moment, the ritual is a way for me to express my connection to Fire through acknowledging my relationship to my beloved sun-star, around which I revolve as does Earth and all beings living on her. And then again, I spin on my internal axis: an abiding oneness with my Creator, in a circular dance of life choreographed by great mysteries. You could call me a sun worshipper but that would be wrong. It would be more accurate to say that I am in sacred relationship with the source of my life here on Earth, itself an embodiment of the Divine.

There, close to the flames, a powerful resurgence of memory and experience is initiated, arriving at the forefront of my awareness like a flash flood. These are living fragments informed by recalled bloodlines reminding themselves into my life at this moment. I am called to acknowledge my richly cast ancestry and to broaden the inner and outer circumference of where I see my place in this world and my life's direction.

As an ageless spirit, I know that I belong to creation itself. I am not defined by one particularity or another and I experience my soul-referenced Self as liberated. But, there is a shadowed sad side to this free spirit: as a culture-bound, sentient being in this world, none has ever embraced me fully as one of their own kind. There is a level of cultural engagement, involvement, and identity with others that has always eluded me.

I have worked diligently all my life to have this not matter. I take great pride in being a solitary, in being perfectly at ease in my own company whether I am, in fact, completely alone or in the midst of a great gathering. At the same time, because I am a multinational, because I am a multivalent being, I have all the while become too much of the *outsider* at a level too deep for me to reach. And, with what is happening to me now, I must go there in order to elicit the softening or pliability needed for a necessary shift that I suspect Fire is calling me to make. I don't necessarily want to do this.

Culturally speaking, I have always seen myself as more of an invited guest wherever I may be, even in my own family circle, and the archetypal presence that constellates to my side is that of the enigmatic visitor: a welcome guest for a limited time only. *I cannot decide to belong to one or another culture because, being multiethnic, I am not perceived by any of the cultures with whom I identify by blood and by spirit as being fully one of their own.*

Feminist scholar Gloria Anzaldua calls this a borderland state of mind. It is an in between place, neither here nor there in concrete, lived terms. Please don't get me wrong. Living in the borderlands, walking out onto the edge of things to enjoy unobstructed views is exhilarating, liberating, and incredibly empowering. At the same time, it is profoundly isolating. This country called Borderland is an ephemeral, floating world. I will never know the sense of unquestioned belonging that a full-blood Japanese, Indian, Swedish, English, or Bantu tribeswoman knows.

This life-long complex, normally held in check effectively, has constellated unexpectedly and dramatically as I prepare for and participate in the Fire ritual.

Roots too strong and too deep to be nourished by anything but unmixed bloodlines are something I know about on an intuitive soul level but have never experienced in the everydayness of my life, this time around. Instead, I am a seasonal migration. At any given time I can be welcomed temporarily or shunned prejudicially depending on the person, group, community, or culture. If there is an invitation, the welcome may last days, weeks, or even years. Meanwhile, never losing sight of the fact that I am only a guest, I explore, hunt, gather provisions, and move on when the time is right.

There is a certain kind of strength, centeredness, focus, and even power in living under the sway of the visitor archetype. As there is an immense Self-knowing underscored by a deeply generative, sustaining and more generous wisdom. I experience it as a kind of radiant heat within my belly that cooks stuff otherwise inedible even poisonous into nourishment. It is a Fire in my soul that, in spite of everything, keeps me forever oriented to the Light and to my origin in the Divine.

Fire is unpredictable and dangerous, a destroyer. It is the tool chest of Armageddon. We never know what will be pried open, scalded, split down the middle, crushed at the root, or cracked open as seeds are when kissed by the running flames of a wildfire. But Fire is also a regenerative force. It signifies the abiding comfort of hearth and home, a safe haven, and is a guarantor of life.

As I make offerings to the flames, I confess the long unacknowledged and taught humiliation concerning certain strains of ancestral blood that runs through my veins to my Fire sisters. Individuals who have suffered overt racial prejudice know this. We know that shame is a heated emotion that, if applied with enough of the right kind of pressure, can shrink the boldest heart, forcing her to her knees. At the same time, Fire invites me to honor the timeless existence of my own Self. It is a moment of power to be witnessed by Earth-in-her-Angel, all the invoked beings present and accounted for, and my beloved Fire sisters.

Tears fall and words tumble into the smoke-scented blue air as I step even closer to the flames, cradling in both hands a solid orb of lapis lazuli. My sisters, feeling the depth of the moment, spontaneously rise from their chairs and draw close, taking up sentinel positions marking each of the four cardinal directions. They hold me energetically in an intimate field of loving concern.

My childhood years were spent in the world of the British Raj in India, which became Pakistan in the late 1950's. Today, by the Fire, I weep strong tears. I share my abiding sorrow over the loss of my East Indian heritage because of the mortification it carried for my Anglo-Eurasian-Indian mother. She forbade any identification with it once we returned to England after India had won her independence from Great Britain.

As a devout Roman Catholic, who spent the formative years of her childhood in a Muslim country, I had to keep secret my respectful awe of Allah, and the intense, sacred joy, the immediate stillness in the soul that I would experience at hearing the *muezzin* sing out the Call to Prayer five times a day all over the city. I sing it even today though I am not a Muslim in the traditional sense of the term.

I also honored Brahma, Vishnu, and all the minor Hindu deities and nature spirits from the start and gave my heart long ago to Lord Krishna and Devi. I loved their stories as much as I loved Hans Christian Andersen's tales and all the stories of saints and sinners that the nuns crippled our innocent minds with at the Catholic Convent School. I learned to love all of God in every image or sound that bespoke sacred presence. Meanwhile, living with the weight of this terrible hypocrisy, I clung fervently to the Catholic High Mass that I sang devotedly in Latin every Sunday in spite of my instinctive and growing disbelief in most of the Catholic precepts being forced into my persistently inquiring child's mind.

I was the victim of cane beatings at the hands of the nuns and the priests throughout my young years at Catholic School because I dared to question and then outright reject what seemed to me to be illogical and contrary beliefs. How could Jesus suffer all little children to come to him and then condemn all those who had no way of knowing he even existed to a terrifying place called Limbo—forever? Where was the love of God there? Even as a small child, I believed much too earnestly in a truly all loving, which by my definition meant all inclusive, and compassionate God. I refused to believe the stuff and nonsense fed to us on a daily basis.

I also understood very early the price one had to pay to stand on the *outside* of things in order to live and function courageously from the Self's own position of intuitively revealed truth. From the point of view of the Catholic Church, it was nothing less than having to personally accept the probability of hell and eternal torment. However, for what I knew then and still know in my Self to be true, I have no choice but to skirt the edge of damnation.

Here by the roaring flames, and wrapped in blue smoke shot with sunlight, what has been constellated for me is the complex, bittersweet experience of ruptured identity. There is a constant tug-of-war between my borderland personality and the part of me still not reconciled to the fact that I will never know, in this lifetime, the depth and joy of a singular cultural identification that I witness in others. When I see this played out in art and literature, poetry and patriotism, in the great cultural and social movements of the world, and on the silver screen it moves me to pathos and grief.

I am surprised and shocked because, in my deepest, inner sense of Self, I am solidly centered. I know who I am and where I am going. Always have. Yet, at another level, I both suffer and celebrate my borderlander ethos. I am an intimate of the outsider archetype. This is what Fire has invited me to bring to the ritual: revisit, explore, and work my borderlander complex. In order to do this I must create a new cultural clearing within myself where I will be able to explore and reclaim an aspect of my Self that I have taken for granted but that clearly needs tending.

As discussed earlier, Jung would describe this kind of soul work as taking the position of holding the inner tension between the opposites and successfully negotiating the tension between one's own contradictions toward a final resolution.

Over the years of growing into womanhood and then as a young adult, I have also cultivated a great love for Mother India all the way back to Vedic times. Here, by the Fire's blaze, I ritually offer lovingly prepared saffron rice cooked in milk and sugar to the dancing flames, all the while calling in the beloved presences of Shiva and his Shakti manifested as she is in a glory of goddesses: Parvati, Durga, and Kali Ma to name just a few.

I cry out to my abandoned ancestors of the Hindu Kush, asking them to turn toward me that we might mutually welcome each other at a soul level and share with each other our Selves, our wisdom traditions, the welcome weight of our karmic responsibilities in this world and in worlds to come. I invite them to bless my children and all our genetically linked descendants with the beauty and intelligence, soul and strength of our hidden bloodlines.

I weep again for the fact that I will never fully belong to my beloved English, Celtic, and Norse heritage. I am an Anglo-Eurasian-Indian, not fully one or the other. I am a mongrel, an alien to peoples, cultures, and histories that run in my blood nevertheless like a morning mist curling around a clear mountain stream, or a lightning strike on the rainbow run to the Gates of Valhalla. I offer wild rosemary, white sage, and then heather and silver birch branches to the flames for the World Tree, Yggdrasill, my beloved goddess Freyja, and great Father Odin who keeps me in stride. They stand by me, "holding" my body steady as it begins to gravitate too close to the leaping flames crying out for body contact. They whisper promises of secrets kept and personal companionship.

Suddenly, a change in the wind, a fall of golden oak leaves all around, and the urgent reach of the flames to sear my flesh eases. I feel an inward shift in orientation. My tears become nectar to my lips in the same way that gratitude is a sweet, sweet feeling. Tears flow for the gift of welcome into the indigenous traditions of the peoples of North and Central America. I thank my Native American elders, teachers, and the Great Spirit for the profound gifts of Earth-referenced spirituality and wisdom, the gift of teachings about the strength and beauty found in humility, hard work, and the very real privilege of being ranked last in line. But, more than that, I am thankful for the gift of learning the ancient ways of prayerfully embracing Earth as Mother, herself a source of creation, and of acknowledging the Divine in *all* living things.

My tears continue to fall in the knowing that, as with all others, in this community I too am simply an honored guest, seated for just a while in their gracious company and generous hearts. I will remain a stranger in a strange land no matter how steadfastly and truly welcomed. Revering these traditions, I offer tobacco and sweet grass to the Fire.

My Fire sisters are captivated and weep with me. In response, I deepen my sharing of what I am experiencing. I tell them of the trauma of living in two worlds as a child. On the one hand, I was a fourth generation British *chota memsahib* (little Lady) with the colonized world at her feet as it were. On the other, in England, I was a poor little pakkie mongrel, a darkie, a dirty little wog, and this in a country and culture I had been brought up to identify wholeheartedly as mine, body and soul. It is this contradicted aspect of my personal history that is unfolding anew in my present tense with Fire, Earth-in-her-Angel, my Fire Sisters, Grandmother Oak, and all the world surrounding.

I talk about growing up as a child struggling to develop a cultural self identity that would engage and become authentically involved wherever and with whomever I might be, while the back-story tells of a young, prepubescent girl being used and abused by a variety of men of many races. In the ensuing contamination, I knew by definition that I would be automatically disenfranchised in a Catholic world that values purity and the virgin principle in women above all others.

I confess myself to my sisters and to my spirit community now drawn so close that their particular fragrances enrich my senses. I share how, on the outside of things, growing up as a solitary child, and into my teenage years, I was called an unbearable snob, accused of having a princess complex, as being strange, unpredictable, depressed, dark, and sometimes just plain frightening. Well, much of that is true. I carried heavy weight after all. I was and still am, in many ways, a natural born heretic, blasphemous, and according to some, the Devil's own advocate.

Yet, it is also in the heart of that portrayal that the solid core of the threefold woman I am today: me, my Self, and I, was forged. Thank God for God when I needed divine intervention to catch my fall into the abyss. St. Joan of Arc was sent in visions to my bedside on the first night of the first dark touch to teach this helpless innocent the art of spiritual warfare. She taught me of the soul's armor, her special weaponry forged in the Fires of righteous rage, and what I can only call "tricks of the trade" from the avenging Self's future vantage point. St. Joan is still my finest teacher and mentor and my debt to her is eternal. Finally, as a young woman coming into my own feminine power, I hit back for all it was worth. It was not a pretty sight. Men were not happy.

Ritual offerings again feed and fan the flames as they rise and curl, spinning into a miniature tornado caught up in the white heart of the Fire. I talk with my Fire sisters about the importance of not ignoring the opposing side of things when approaching or engaging with the Divine: another lesson learned well.

I give thanks for the long-suffering wisdom of that darkly radiant and beloved archangel Lucifer, another careful and loyal sage. It was he who taught me from the start how to think about evil with my *soul's intelligence* even while helplessly gripped in its vice. It's about fighting Fire with Fire.

I invite the sisters to remember that our truest enemy is fear. And, that rather than fearing the enemy, it is best to get to know him/her/it as well and as intimately as possible. We cannot tame, fight, defeat, or destroy the thing we fear for it is fear itself that guarantees our enemy victory!

Now, the wind spins upward and the sky is shot through with shards of bright blue shining between thunderheads closing in. I thank Earth-in-her-Angel for providing a sane and safe haven from it all as throughout my life I have continued with the soul work that is mine and mine alone to carry out.

Here, by the Fire, I look back over the ensuing adult years of intensive spiritual practice and self analysis; of gifting this world with two amazing children now grown; of learning slowly and painfully how to create lasting friendships; and of participating in a healthy community life. I confess to my Fire sisters my great surprise at the stunning reappearance of this borderlander complex that I thought no longer relevant. I had shelved it safely away inside the secret recesses of my own being years ago. But here it is, suddenly and so powerfully proclaiming its presence in my mind, my body, my emotions, and my soul.

As I stand for a long moment in meditative silence by the now quietly burning flames, a familiar and well-beloved insight crystallizes. When we commit to this kind of soul work, with the goal being wholeness and Self-integration, we sign up for a lifetime of recurrences. It is a holy quest of epic proportion that has no linear ending. You see, we all return again and again to the thing still not fully reconciled, still needing to be tended to from another vantage point, or needing to be viewed and understood differently, this time.

Accordingly, here with Fire by my side, I am transported into my own inner world, to a metaphorical dimension that mirrors my outer experience. I am standing at the border, at a crossroads: a threshold. I am a visitor in the inner landscape of my own soul peopled with self-aspects who live and function interiorly. Gloria Anzaldua's calls this "a consciousness of the borderlands, or *mestiza* consciousness … where the phenomena tend to collide. It is where the possibility of uniting all that is separate, occurs." "The work," she says, "takes place underground—subconsciously. It is the work the soul performs."

Once again, after all these many years, I have to face and interact with that aspect of myself that I identify as the mongrel, mediating the core antagonism between the reality of my mixed blood: not belonging, versus something I will never know, being a pureblood: belonging. Of course I understand that the concept of pure bloodedness is fundamentally flawed. There is probably no such thing in point of fact. There is, however, the very real lived experience that marks an individual's irrefutable sense of belonging to a people, a place, and a history in profoundly permanent ways.

As I allow myself to draw deeper into the affect of my own emotion around the flames, I realize that I have unconsciously created a dynamic of colonized self versus colonizing self. I have colonized my own multiethnic, culturally, and spiritually diverse self-aspects who have, in turn, succumbed to the belief system that "we" are fundamentally inferior; therefore, by definition, only worthy of a nominal temporary welcome wherever we may be. The tears continue all the while, now like a rushing river caught up in a boulder-strewn cross current, now winding with the slow pace of sweet water settled into the deeps.

We know from Jung that in as much as polarity is inherent in all living things, "nothing so promotes the growth of consciousness as [the] inner confrontation of opposites." And I am being called out to do just this. Fire has asked me to step out and disclose this wounded self-aspect. I need to give voice to my own need for integration in this particular respect. This is the process of individuation revealed. Here in the arbor at Indian Canyon, as a participant in a Fire ritual, it unfolds for me as a personal experience of rupture, regression, resistance, re-evaluation, and redemption.

Jungian analyst Helene Lorenz reminds us, "Because the individuation process requires a confrontation with the Shadow, and a 'defeat of the ego,' nothing in the past can help us to predict what call may suddenly be felt. We have to be open for what brings us joy, excitement and energy or pain, sadness and a blockage in the new landscape, and enter into a deep dialogue with it."

Here in the arbor, surrounded by natural beauties, encircled by altars and symbolic objects, I tend to and feed the Fire, and understand that this day I need to be both the originator and mediator of my own process of reconciliation with regard to this particular life stance.

It begins with permitting an injured self-aspect to be drawn out and placed at the forefront of my consciousness. Then I must name it, knowing that to identify a problem accurately is critical to connecting its symptoms with its cause. I must make a visceral connection between my borderlander complex and the emotional and psychological trauma that is its source.

Aurora Morales reminds: "What is so dreadful is that to transform the traumatic we must re-enter it fully, and allow the full weight of grief to pass through our hearts." She insists that, "what is required to face trauma is the ability to mourn, fully and deeply, all that has been taken from us." Again, "only through mourning everything we have lost can we discover that we have in fact survived; that our spirits are indestructible."

I move into my own place of deep insight and receptivity to vision. Something is surfacing and being brought into focus on a conscious level. There is a need to intensify my interaction with this beloved, always enigmatic archetype, the visitor, in relationship to my borderlander complex. I see that it has repositioned itself once again in my awareness, and, as a result of the soul work at hand, the archetype itself is moving toward a critical shift in orientation and purpose with regard to my life and *its* ongoing role in it.

Again, I am transported into a vision. I close my eyes and move even closer to Fire until I feel the heat sear my flesh and smell the burn in my hair. I open my "inner eyes" and see that the small, oak-encircled arbor is filled with people I recognize as deceased family members, and even farther back, sense to be my ancestors. They are accompanied by children I know to be mine from lives past, and who are descendants still to come.

I feel compelled by the orange-gold flames and the white smoke curling around my body like the double helix of a DNA strand to continue my story. The Fire sisters draw even closer to me as I move ever more deeply into the pain of my abiding sense of alienation. The irony, of course, is that I do this in the spiritual presence of hundreds of beings here precisely because I do belong to them! My abiding love for the peculiarly exquisite beauty that lives in the heart of paradox remains present.

My borderlander self emerges into the light, making herself known in the ways archetypes constellating around a complex usually do: in the poetic images, tears falling like rain on golden ground, in spiritual visitations, in the exaggerated language of myth, and from the ground on up. As the visions begin to take an alchemical turn, I am reminded that the key to holding steady is to keep it real. I am always careful to approach Fire as an initiate, or, from a Zen Buddhist perspective, in a state of *mushin* or beginner's mind. Humility is the correct stance. It keeps the rest of one's personhood intact.

I feel a sudden gravitational pull and an urgent desire to fall into the flames like a newborn planet caught in the grip of its own sun before it falls into its own ellipse. I must stand strong. Something arises within me layering out like silk chiffon the way a dawn mist appears in some distant wild place. Suddenly, like a wild creature released from a trap, I experience the deliverance of a lifetime of living inside my own borderlander complex. Catching my breath as the flames crack and explode, I open my eyes to see white butterflies fluttering all around. Are they actually dancing with the flames? Is it done?

I wonder what my colonizing and colonized selves will do? Where will they go, and even more cautiously, *who* will arrive to take up residence in the empty spaces left behind? We tend to hoard and cherish our own complexes. After all, they are like a home away from home. There is safety in the known and the familiar.

I remember the salamander and the lapis lazuli. These two powerfully evocative images tell me there is alchemy and magic on the loose, and I must surrender fearlessly to the force of it. A personal totem for many years, I search for the salamander in the glowing embers.

How interesting—the synchronicity of things. On *this* day, early in the morning, as John and I prepared the ritual site, a beautiful salamander, the color of dusky rose made its appearance, crawling out from under the damp logs stacked up by the fire pit. I was thrilled as I gently picked her up and cradled her in the palm of my hand. She looked shyly up at me as I smiled, welcoming her to the ritual setting.

We walked together around the site, and I quietly spoke with her about everything we were about to engage in this day. What is spectacular about salamanders is that they really *look* at you in the most knowing and intelligent way. They watch and listen as a human would, quietly, thoughtfully. And, they are incredibly feeling creatures. They emanate a tender, steady passion, a unique kind of unadulterated love.

The salamander remained in my hand willingly, walking back and forth up to my forearm and back to my palm. She turned round to gaze into my eyes as I talked to her, and only after I had carefully placed her on the ground on the outer boundaries of the arbor did she crawl slowly back into the welcoming damp of the dark undergrowth.

For the medieval alchemists, salamander symbolically represented the indestructible Self. I often wonder if any of them actually sat down and conversed with salamanders. Did they bask in the tender sensation of their warm and moist bodies treading gently and carefully on human skin? Did these mystical chemists of old marvel at the soft and deeply expressive eyes that intelligently appraised their faces? Did they understand why salamanders, as Earth beings in their own right, are as magical, holy, and precious, every one of them, as their alchemical counterparts in the world of symbol and the creative imagination?

In her archetypal form, for me this day, while I speak from my own heart to the heart of the Fire, I see salamander in the form of a dancing flame slowly curving upwards around the fragrant burning logs. Intently watching me at each turn, shimmering in her gradual ascent, as I come to the end of my own soul's outpouring, she slowly disappears into the coiling spirals of blue smoke shot with rays of gold from the sun.

Salamander signifies the enduring aspect of the fully individuated Self. By the term enduring, I do not mean to imply fixedness. I do not believe in notions of permanence, rigidity, or containment when they refer to the soul's journey, itself a reflection of an eternally expanding and recurring process of creation. I believe that the Self, in the face of seemingly impossible suffering and loss, can nevertheless endure the most profound changes without being deprived of the essential integrity of its true nature.

According to alchemy, salamander symbolizes the manifest Self in its capacity to endure *without faltering. This* quality is stronger than Fire. Metaphorically speaking, salamander may enter Fire, be reduced to charcoal, pitch black yet graced with a certain radiant sheen, and rise reborn out of the ashes, whole once again displaying the dusky deep rose of a new dawn.

I have always been an introverted and deeply exploratory woman in terms of my own inner life. Archetypal psychologist Carol Pearson describes the function of the wanderer archetype, typically twinned with the visitor, as agent, producer, and creator. She insists, "No matter how much people want to feel loved, appreciated, and a part of things, there will be a loneliness deep in their souls until they make a commitment to themselves, a commitment that is so total that they will give up community and love, if necessary, to be fully who they are."

I will follow salamander into the inferno. It is where I belong. I will stay true to my own solitary Self quietly ablaze at the edge of the world. Yes, I have learned how to belong authentically, just for a moment in time, and then I move on. I am a pilgrim making my own way toward a sacred destination. I stop for a while wherever I am welcomed for rest, recuperation, and nourishment along the way. I belong to my own Divine source of existence where my true home is. I have boon companions. They will escort me home. It is ALL good.

As I move toward completing my own rites with Fire, the flood of tears finally stops with my last gift offerings, invocations, praises and thanksgivings. Close to the blaze that has already singed my eyebrows and burnt strands of my hair, I stand tall and strong, celebrating the fierce independence and strength of heart that has been my gift from early childhood, directly as a result of having to accept my *outsider-other* status. As I sprinkle olive oil mixed with honey and handfuls of fresh rosemary sprigs onto the flames, I give thanks for the particular magnetic power within me that shows itself as an enigma to others yet serves as an inner anchor for me wherever I am. I am grateful for the strange, dignified beauty of the visitor archetype that has become my familiar.

As I gaze into the violet-trimmed flames, I see even more clearly this great archetype that stories itself through me as I do through it. In the deepest sense of things, I *know* that I am here in this life simply to visit. I am to take in the sights and sounds, to witness, to carry out certain tasks prescribed in the great mystery of things, to love much, and to be even kinder still. I offer my gratitude to all beings, sentient and in spirit, who have accompanied me in the preparation of and during the Fire ritual. It is to them that I offer my final gifts of honey, wild mint, and healing water taken from an ancient waterfall in Indian Canyon. A sacred chant rises up through me and sings itself out, filling the air.

Over the next days and weeks after the Fire ritual, I began to process my experience. I was called to undergo a severe and unexpectedly painful reunion with a persona buried years ago. I also had to admit a certain kind of suffering that I have comfortably endured over time because of its familiarity. I was surprised at the intensity of the breakdown and of the depth of grieving that arose from somewhere so deep, somewhere so well hidden.

I had imagined myself fully reconciled, healthy, and strong with a life lived as what I call a "universal being." I was beyond race, ethnicity, culture, or needing to have a sense of rootedness to place: a citizen of the world. This in spite of my experience living in the borderland, at least in terms of understanding that I will never know what it is to fully belong by blood to a *particular* people, culture, and history. I continue to be amazed at how much that still means to me.

My experience demanded a response wrung from the bowels where, as the ancient Greeks knew, great passions, and the wounds of the heart reside, festering and smoldering until tended. Intellectually, philosophically, and spiritually, I know and experience my soul-referenced Self beyond this borderlander complex. But somewhere alchemically calcified in my bones; somewhere, lying like a hibernating Fire dragon in the double-helixed formula of my own blood ways is a crying need simply to go home to a people who will recognize and embrace me as fully one of their own.

Simultaneous to the beautiful vision of my ancestors and descendants and the experience of being accompanied by nature spirits, powerful deities, and Earth-in-her-Angel, was the deep fall into the heart of my own Shadow. There, the darkest memories surfaced, and a long-muzzled righteous rage needing to be sounded out.

As had happened with each of my Fire sisters, my formally stated intention to participate in the Fire ritual triggered the reemergence of an old injury around which the borderlander complex had built itself a home. In ritually engaging with Fire, I was compelled to take a backward glance while examining the moment at hand and its contents, not just deeply, but also imaginatively. I had to reach ground zero where a new beginning awaited in the interstices between the heart, the mind, the body, and the soul. I walk now with my borderlander complex in hand, caring for it, honoring it as righteous. I look for the dignity and nobility it contains and I understand it will last at least for this lifetime.

EPILOGUE

I WANTED TO show in this book how Earth offers her own Self as an authentic alchemical container within which we may tend to our own soul-referenced Selves. Creating and sustaining recurring ritual-based interactions with her can be critical to the process of discovering and uniting all aspects of our selves to form an integrated, centered and illuminated Self. This inner work calls for a peripheral consciousness that takes into account the constant, loving, and active consideration of Earth-in-her-Angel in all her myriad forms.

Using the dynamic framework of an Earth-centered sacramental ritual as an example, I wanted to show how Jungian depth psychology, in particular, can do its most transformative work for the individual, for the culture, and the natural world in which we live. I hoped too, that this book would illustrate the power of Earth as the wondrous and intelligent being she is in her own right when her particular orientation toward an individual is articulated in terms of rescue, restoration, restructuring, and healing.

As we revisit the Fire sister's works in these concluding remarks, I believe that they illustrate this beautifully. We each found ourselves caught up in a constellation of several personal and collective complexes that activated almost immediately. We each fell headlong into our abyss, and our textual works are a testament to the intensity of our engagement with the individuation process as it revealed itself in the weeks leading up to and during our participation in the Fire ritual. It was clear to all of us, as we acknowledged each other's personal Fire rite and shared our experiences, that we were already in the process of living deeply transforming lives that drew equally from the treasured dimensions of the darkness within and from the sun-kissed, and beautifully ordered light of day.

I invited each Fire sister, prior to the ritual, to pray, envision, or, if they were familiar with the Jungian practice of creative imagination, to use that technique in a series of meditations whose purpose was to invoke and bring to light Fire in its archetypal or spirit form. Once an image appeared and made contact, each sister was to engage in continuous communication with it over the ensuing weeks regarding the preparation phase and the actual rite itself. In this case, it was Spirit in its form as Fire who was being looked to as therapist, teacher, healer, and archetypal presence. I encouraged us all to open ourselves to experience a special kind of generosity of heart, an *eros consciousness* that would allow for a variety of unique expressions of the process of individuation as it articulated for each of us within the context of this one holy rite.

I wondered whether a sense of deep and enduring unity could be created and sustained in the heart of the ritual in spite of the varying activities, multicultural symbolism, and uniquely personal issues that each woman brought to it. As both the facilitator of and participant in the Fire ritual, this was an important consideration for me. Many Earth-centered rites I am aware of, whether ancient or current, are strictly representative of a culturally specific cosmology replete with its own symbol traditions, laden in turn with their own particular significances and meanings. I wondered, with some measure of anxiety, as to whether our ritual engagement with Earth, with our own inner Selves, and with each other would be diminished because it lacked a specific cultural uniformity: a shared body of sacred teachings and wisdom traditions.

I had to trust in my own vision and guidance. I needed to stay true to the inspiration and the instructions regarding the Fire ritual imparted to me by Fire and other entities. During the ritual and in the Fire texts offered by the sisters, I was gratified to observe that the resonant and effectual power of the Fire ritual as a container for the Divine in *all* its culturally variegated manifest forms was as powerfully transforming as any strictly prescribed culturally informed ritual I have had the privilege to participate in.

The Fire sisters approached the ritual in ways unique to our own vision, poetic reverie, and soul stance.

During the ritual, we were witnesses to the actualization of our own preliminary processes of preparation as we began to carry out our own rites in a fourfold dynamic, each according to her inspired instructions. Each Fire sister became for the others a reflective image, and a presence strong enough to hold on to as we engaged intimately and sometimes too closely with Fire in full force. We carefully and protectively watched each other disintegrate in the face of the roaring flames and wept in joy during moments of reintegration.

Fire as the Divine embodied was an illumination in and of itself, gifting each of us with new and deeper levels of Self knowledge. In this way, the human soul opens to the soul of the world, to Earth-in-her-Angel, in a mutual embrace that simultaneously expresses the rapture of the deep connection and the terrible beauty of the pathos and pain involved. Each one of us had to fully accept her imperfections, her own wounded Self.

We listened to, held, supported, and empowered each other, and became a community of women who are now unafraid of Fire. We can build it, feed it, and tend to its needs.

This work was derived from, inspired, and sustained by an Earth vision given to me by the "Angel" in her. It is for and about Earth-in-her-Angel voicing her Self through my Self in very particular ways. It is also about four women who have a peculiar affinity and affiliation with the natural world. For us, Earth *is* the Garden of Eden, and we are already in Paradise. She is the means, one of many, by which the Divine speaks to us in the everyday.

In her Angel, Earth insists that we dig deeper into each image that appears on the surface of our consciousness. She demands the lifting of the veils that hide the darkest iniquities, secret raptures and sins that, like the scales on the skin of a strangely beautiful silver serpent, coil around our hearts and minds like a dark enchantment. She will stand rock solid by any wounded woman unafraid to embrace the paradox in her own soul.

The Fire ritual proved to be an extraordinarily profound experience for us all. We each talked about and freely enacted whatever was occurring for us on a soul level, in our bodies, and in our thinking. We responded to the invitation to cultivate a *thinking heart* that knows the names of the souls of things. We encouraged gods and goddesses and other spirit entities, ancestors, and Earth to the table that we might feast together. We remained unafraid of the voices inside our heads, of the Shadow, the fall, and the abyss.

To continue the work, I suggest we need to take it out to the streets, to the ocean's edge, to the forest glade, to a Zen garden, to a women's circle, to a children's playground, to a homeless shelter. We need to think, feel, and become the things of this world. We need to recognize that this ground we stand on is the true point of our actual origins. We did not emerge as a species on a star. We were generated out of the life-giving substance of this ground—the ground of a wondrously beautiful blue planet that exists in relation to and because of a glorious golden star. We are earth beings, human by nature, sacred, and instilled with spirit by the breath of the Divine.

We need to feel the deepest empathy for this Mother of all creatures, to fiercely love and protect her as once we did, and to safeguard her very life from our own species, her greatest danger. In this one particular case, we cannot afford to commit matricide. After all, her survival is our survival.

SUGGESTED READING

Anzaldua, G. (2007). *Borderlands/La Frontera: The New Mestiza*. San Francisco, CA: Aunt Lute Books.

Bachelard, G. (1964b). *The Psychoanalysis of Fire*. Boston, MA: Beacon Press.

Bane, R. (1999). *Dancing in the Dragon's Den: Rekindling the Creative Fire in your Shadow*. York Beach, ME: Nicolas-Hays, Inc.

D. A. Brading. (2001). *Mexican Phoenix: Our Lady of Guadalupe*. Cambridge University Press.

Brown, Joseph Epes. (1984). *The Sacred Pipe: Black Elk's Account of the Seven Rites of the Oglala Sioux*. New York, NY: Penguin Books.

Corbett, L. (1996). *The Religious Function of the Psyche*. New York, NY: Routledge.

Corbin, H. (1977). *Spiritual Body and Celestial Earth: From Mazdean Iran to Shi'ite Islam*. Princeton, NJ: Princeton University Press.

Duerr, P. (1985). *Dreamtime: Concerning the Boundary Between Wilderness and Civilization*. New York, NY: Basil Blackwell.

Ely, R., Anodea, J. (1992). Pinnacles National Monument. In F. Joseph (Ed.), *Sacred sites*. St. Paul, MN: Llewellyn Publications.

Emerson, R. W. (1981). Nature. In C. Bode, M. Cowley. (Eds.), *The Portable Emerson*. New York, NY: Viking Penguin.

Goodchild, V. (2013). *Songlines of the Soul: Pathways to a New Vision for a New Century*. Santa Barbara, CA: Academy of Imaginal Studies, Books.

Hamilton, E. (1942). *Mythology: Timeless Tales of Gods and Heroes*. New York, NY: The New American Library.

Hillman, J. (1981). *The Thought of the Heart and the Soul of the World*. Woodstock, CT: Spring Publications.

Hyde, L. (1979). *The Gift: Imagination and the Erotic Life of Property*. New York, NY: Vintage Books.

Jacobi, J. (1959). *Complex, Archetype, Symbol, in the Psychology of C. G. Jung*. New York, NY: Princeton University Press.

Jung, C. G. (1959). *Memories, Dreams, Reflections*. New York, NY: Random House.

Jung, C. G. (1969). On the Nature of the Psyche. In R. F. C. Hull (Trans.), *The Collected Works of C. G. Jung* (Vol. 8). Princeton, NJ: Princeton University Press. (Original work published 1960)

Lorenz, H. (2000). The Presence of Absence: Mapping Post-colonial

Spaces. In L. Corbett and D. Slattery (Eds.), *Depth Psychology: Meditations From the Field*. Einsiedlen, Switzerland: Daimon Verlag.

Murdock, M. (2000). Telling our Stories: Making Meaning from Myth and Memoir. In D. Slattery & L. Corbett (Eds.), *Depth Psychology: Meditations From the Field*. Einseidlen, Switzerland: Daimon Verlag.

Naess, A. (1988). Self Realization: An Ecological Approach to Being-in-the-World. In J. Seed, P. Fleming, J. Macy, & A. Naess (Eds.), *Thinking like a Mountain: Towards a Council of All Beings* (pp. 19-30). Philadelphia, PA: New Society.

Paris, G. (1986). *Pagan Meditations: The Worlds of Aphrodite, Artemis, Hestia*. Woodstock, CT: Spring Publications.

Pinkola Estés, C. (1992). *Women Who Run With the Wolves: Myths and Stories of the Wild Woman Archetype*. New York, NY: Ballantine Books.

Raff, J. (2000). *Jung and the Alchemical Imagination*. Berwick, ME: Nicolas-Hays.

Rockwell, D. (1991). *Giving voice to the Bear: North Native American Myths, Rituals and Images of the Bear*. Niwot, CO: Robert Rhinehart.

Romanyshyn, R. (1999). *The Soul in Grief: Love, Death and Transformation*. Berkeley, CA: Frog.

Schwartz-Salant, N. (Ed.). (1995). *Jung on Alchemy*. Princeton, NJ: Princeton University Press.

Slattery, D. (2000). *The Wounded Body: Remembering the Markings of Flesh*. Albany, NY: State University of New York Press.

Thorsson, E. (1987). *Runelore: A Handbook of Esoteric Runology*. York Beach, ME: Samuel Weisler.

Turner, V. (Ed.). (1974). Pilgrimages as Social Processes. In *Dramas, Fields, and Metaphors: Symbolic Action in Human Society*. Ithaca, NY: Cornell University Press.

von Franz, M. -L. (1964). The Process of Individuation. In C. G. Jung and M.-L. von Franz (Eds.), *Man and his Symbols*. New York, NY: Doubleday & Company.

INDEX

www.ingramcontent.com/pod-product-compliance
Lightning Source LLC
Chambersburg PA
CBHW030314290526
45785CB00001B/355